Creativity in Dance

Endpapers:
Moving Lines   *Photograph: Robert Walker*
Opposite: Coralie Hinkley

Creativity in Dance

by

Coralie Hinkley

*An imaginative source of creative work for the teaching of
dance in education as an Expressive Art Form*

Alternative Publishing Co-operative Limited,
10 Shepherd Street, Chippendale, Sydney

No part of this work may be
reproduced without written permission

First published 1980

Alternative Publishing Co-operative Limited
Sydney, Australia

© Coralie Hinkley

ISBN 0 909188 16 5; paper, 24 6

Printed by Hogbin, Poole (Printers) Pty. Ltd, Redfern, N.S.W. 2016

TO THE MEMORY OF MY MOTHER AND FATHER

Thematic Material in Dance from my Teaching Experiences at

FORT STREET GIRLS' HIGH SCHOOL—1963–1974

FORT STREET HIGH SCHOOL—1975

Sydney—Australia

"Content labour is the Law of ART as well as the law of life, for ART is the creative activity of the mind.

AND there results a habit of toil, a perpetual consciousness of the difficulties, that keeps them in a state of marriage with the Muse, and her creative forces".

—Balzac

"I want Poets Declared Equal to . . ."

"There's nothing I want for my country more than ART—artists poets".

Robert Frost, American poet; from his speech in 1960, speaking in support of a bill to create a National Academy of Culture. In his role as honorary consultant in the Humanities to the Library of Congress, he appeared before the Education Sub-Committee of the Senate Committee on Labor and Public Welfare to testify on a bill to create such an academy; the above lines were part of his speech to campaign for this Academy and to stimulate public interest in the arts, and have them declared equal to "Big business, Science and Scholarship".

The New York Times Magazine, May 15, 1960)

O chestnut tree, great rooted blossomer,
Are you the leaf, the blossom or the bole?
O body swayed to music, O brightening glance,
How can we know the dancer from the dance?

—W. B. Yeats

Contents

Acknowledgements

In a life centred around the dance I have several people to whom I owe special gratitude—to my beloved teacher and great artist, Gertrud Bodenwieser,[1] from whom I inherited my knowledge of the modern dance as an expressive art form, and in whose dance company I performed for so many years, enriching my experience as a dancer and teacher in her school; and not least to Sheila Whytock, who shared her dancing spirit with me. For three years I enjoyed, through the assistance of a Fulbright Scholarship, a study programme in the United States with the great teachers and artists of modern dance; Doris Humphrey, Martha Graham, Louis Horst, Merce Cunningham and Mary Anthony. With them, I found the idea of dance that I had always believed in, functioning with the highest aesthetic and artistic ideals; with aliveness and vision, and a striving after perfection in their own individualistic movement theories. Through their own personal commitment to the modern or contemporary dance, they all contributed to make my experience of dance as a creative and performing art, momentous.

Furthermore, I am indebted to Dr Gladys Andrews of New York University who directed my thinking towards the role of creativity and its place in education. To Martha Hill of dance division, Juilliard School of Music, my thanks for her interest in the project. Also my appreciation to Helen Palmer for her comments on reading the manuscript and to Denise Fletcher for her encouragement and invaluble assistance during the completion of this project. I would like to hope that some of the ideas expressed in this text will inspire my daughter Sancha during her teaching career.

My gratitude to my Principal, Evelyn Rowe, of Fort Street High School, for her unfailing and helpful support of the work and the recognition of its beneficial influence in the total development of the child.

And lastly a word in praise of the dance spirit of the students at Fort Street; that they may bring their own individual gifts into the community and continue for many years, their own creative process.

---

1 Gertrud Bodenwieser, formerly Professor of Dance and Choreography; Academy of Music and Theatre Arts, Vienna, 1924–1938. The foremost pioneer of modern dance in Australia, 1939–1959.

I

Foreword

Movement is life. Death is the cessation of activity. This book is about the ways of stimulating dance activity. Through physical, mental and spiritual alignment, spontaneous dance can occur. When that happens, even a tiny child can amaze us with the truth of dance.

Coralie Hinkley's word pictures are a key to this spontaneous realm. The word pictures reflected back by her students were the material which was used to develop, first, dances, then dance works, and finally dancers.

Creativity is a struggle. The wrestling with one's own inertia which is always necessary if one is to bring down from airy realms an idea or an ideal and put it into freshly improvised visibility and then into a more permanent form—this work is made inviting by the author through her own enthusiasm. Most of us neglect or stifle ideas that are only dimly "felt"—so the achievement of a worthwhile work—the created entity which is a dance, a poem or a painting is still-born from lack of perseverance.

In the class work, and in the advanced session for her special group of dancers, I saw, under Coralie Hinkley's direction, at Fort Street Girls' High School, that the girls were more fully alive because of their creative dance experience. They were more "aware" and a sense of communal inter-communication pervaded their work. Their enthusiasm, and the guidance they received resulted in a technical facility that was both unexpected and a delight. These people had achieved a sense of "giving" not just "getting". Their interest in helping newer and younger dancers was part of Coralie Hinkley's achievement. Her pioneering of Creativity in Dance within the context of an Australian Education Department has resulted in many good things. Not least of these that young people who are stimulated by good training and dedicated teaching can achieve goals approaching professional dance aims, although that was not the main purpose of Coralie Hinkley's work.

The even greater value of her pioneering of dance within the Education Department's school system is seen (in this work) in the perceptive poetry, the intelligent participation and the lucid discussions among the students themselves. But doors have been opened to many more than those whose quotations enliven the pages here. This teacher has pointed a way toward wider concepts of the self and the environment surrounding each child with whom she has worked. That contact is of a lasting value which will carry on through the whole of their lives.

The curiosity inherent in us all has been channelled in this case toward discovery: of poetry, of painting, of literature, and of drama: indeed, discovery that even "everyday things" can become a springboard to creativity. This means that there can be a cohesiveness between interests and studies which promotes education of the whole person during the formative years.

The modern dance of Doris Humphrey was an affirmation, the essence of joy shone in her Brandenburg Concerto choreography. The ideals of Isadora Duncan changed the face of the classical ballet of her time. The path she opened has culminated in the birth of a new classicism, that of Martha Graham.

Modern dance, or contemporary dance as it is sometimes termed, is not the same as ballet dance. Both have developed very powerful and exact techniques, but techniques should be the servants of communication in any art. This does not mean that form is unimportant. Dance really is a language—and some grammar is necessary to any language.

The exciting tension between pristine movement evolved from inner urges and the need for form in which to hold this in order to teach it, to pass it on, refining as we go, is one of the permanent paradoxes in the art of dance. The problem is how to wend our way in our own era.

Today's permissive ways have altered the barriers that once seemed impregnable concerning aesthetic endeavour. But out of amorphous "happenings" and chaotic non sequitur experiments and the non dance trends by dancers, some day another period will crystallise, which will pass away in its turn.

Dance is a performing art. It cannot be expressed fully in the pages of a book. To experience Dance, and to share it together as actual body awareness of movement, is of paramount importance. Book study of Dance alone cannot be the actuality of Dance experience, although it is true that a fine teacher need not necessarily be a star performer. What is necessary for young teachers is to spend time learning the craft of this, or any other art, which they will teach. In Dance, this means doing it (and what could be more appropriate for the age we live in) preferably with a teacher of integrity who has a strong grounding in the whole world of dance.

Creativity, fortunately, is now being fostered in schools in the open classroom context. The main need is for creative teachers—not least in Dance. It is not for every child to reach the peaks of experience in dance, not in life, but few can be left untouched by real sincerity, ability, and dedication. Coralie Hinkley's ideas fired her classes with enthusiasm; they will also stimulate readers of this book. It can help the new generation of teachers to be less wary of the journey into creativity. Creativity can bring such surprises, and joy, when courage and perseverance along with training launch us into the wonder and responsibility of guiding the hearts, minds and bodies of those we teach.

Coralie Hinkley's concepts—those implicit as well as explicit in these pages —will enable other teachers to guide their young charges toward the road leading from an existence which in contemporary context is sometimes sterile, or banal, towards exciting values of lasting merit; the discipline of the arts. Teachers in school must find answers to many problems. Coralie found a solution by, sensibly, not insisting on high technical achievement from the less experienced majority, while giving each participant the valid feeling of movement itself which can be a joyous release. That kind of release is the needed

3

antidote to Blackboard Jungle situations, the dour concrete walls of big cities or—just as stifling to creativity—that narrowed view which little contact with the arts can bring in villages or small towns.

This book has another value to Australians, for it proves that pleasure in movement is not the prerogative of sport alone. Dance is a deeper challenge to the spirit of man, and creativity as a communication of ideas, of ideals, is longer-lasting in its effects than any form of competition.

BETH DEAN
Sydney, January 1978

Introduction

The term "modern dance" has experienced a wide range of meanings. It has been called natural, interpretative, plastique, absolute or contemporary. It has been labelled Creative Dance, dance-drama or expressive dance. This could be due largely to the fact that it is a growing, living, changing art form. Dance for me, means "The Modern Dance". To the dance historian it is "The universal language of Man", "The mother of the Arts". It is man's expression by his instrument, the body, through movement of ideas, emotions and images. The modern dance is the human conception of an idea, or series of ideas made manifest by the use of movement. It has a totally different history and development—language, technique and concept, from classical ballet. Its movement, vocabulary and philosophy is peculiar to its originators.

In the late 19th century and early 20th century, Isadora Duncan, an American, evolved her own theories about dancing. She tried to find a way of dance founded on the law of natural motion and natural rhythms. She experimented with movements and states of feeling and purity of line. She detested the superficial and sterile, in life and in art. It was from this inspiration of Isadora's that the Modern Dance emerged. This idea of a constant search for the freedom to move in a new way has continued up to the present day.

We are the inheritors of a wealth of dance material from the creative minds of individuals from Europe and the United States of America. Some of these outstanding personalities are Mary Wigman, Rosalie Chladek, Hanya Holm, Harold Kreutzberg, Gertrud Bodenwieser, Trudi Schoop, Joos-Leeder and Rudolph von Laban, Denishawn, Charles Weidman, José Limón, Merce Cunningham, Alwin Nikolais, Martha Graham and Doris Humphrey (to mention but a few). From their studios, dancers, teachers and students have come, bringing with them the principles and styles of their dynamic art forms. The dance today is an embodiment of 20th century living, and its tensions, problems and complexities are revealed in its artworks. Now, the younger generation of modern dance artists are driven by their vision to make their statement about man and the space in which he lives. Their keen powers of perception and innovatory skills give their art work a range of expression as wide as life's experience.

Meanwhile, from the 1900s onwards the foundation of dance in education was being laid in Europe with Rudolph von Laban[2] and in the U.S.A. with

2 Laban's theories and principles of movement have been developed in England and are now part of educational dance in schools and in tertiary education.

5

Margaret H'Doubler. These two dance enthusiasts were pushing the question of dance and the basic principles of natural movement. Laban's theories were of time, space and weight and the twenty-sided figure. Icosahedron gave us movements in different planes of space with different nuances of mood and feeling. His theories as we know are responsible for educating us into new ways of movement, new concepts of movement and about orientating movement in space. His theories and practice of movement are taught now throughout the world.

In the United States, Margaret H'Doubler[3] was contributing in the fullest sense towards the growth and acceptance of dance in schools, colleges and universities. Through her inspired teachings and writing, she clarified the meaning of dance. Her writings range from the cultural aspect of dance; creative power; the aesthetic experience; to form and content. She believed that we could all be enriched by an experience in dance and that it should be shared by the child in education. She was aware of the quality values of the dance and of creativity in dance, and believed that it was of the ultimate value in improving the quality of living. Within the structure of the modern dance, two streams of thought and action developed:

Dance as a performing art.

Dance in education.

It is with the latter that I am concerned here.

In dance in education, the growth of the needs and capacities of the individual are extended and enriched. The endowment is directed towards the physical, mental, spiritual, emotional, aesthetic and social attributes of the human being. From movement we can learn about ourselves, our feelings and thoughts and actions. We are made more aware of others and the effect of our own actions on others. We can learn to relate and interact with our fellow man.

Dance sharpens perceptive powers, making us more sensitive to nature and our environment. The critical power of awareness of our sensations is heightened. Human impulses, human values and subsequently behaviour and actions are disciplined and strengthened—we learn to interpret our experiences through dance movement, communicating the inner world of our sub-conscious through a form that is expressive, aiming to evoke a sympathetic response in another person. Dance can be a purely individual matter or it can start a whole new movement. Through movement we seek our creative identity and so assist in the discovery and formation of our individuality and personality. Within the scope of dance is the heightened power of stimulating our imagination. Dance is expressive and creative, and of a compassionate nature. It not only arouses our emotional consciousness but improves the intellectual faculties as our mind learns, receives impressions, selects, manipulates and solves dance problems.

3 *Dance, A Creative Art Experience* by Margaret N. H'Doubler, University of Wisconsin Press.

Our reaction towards the aesthetic experience is deepened, as the relationship of dance with music, poetry, drama, the graphic arts with their sound, colour, shape and form overflow into a creative art activity.   ..

Through dance, the child, if given the opportúnity, can discover the body as an expressive instrument and develop the aesthetic and creative side of its nature. The expression can be a spontaneous thing and can evolve into an individualistic language of movement, providing a satisfying creative experience. All youth needs the experience of dance from primary school onwards— so that they can grow and develop with dance as a natural part of their lives. At all stages of the child's development the creative dance experience leads to a new expressiveness—increased use of the imagination; discovery of new skills in working creatively; an emotional release; increased sensitivity to the environment and to other human beings; deepened aesthetic appreciation. The vital energy for artistic creation is fostered and allowed to flower.

The youngster has much to contribute. It is essential that ideas are listened to and the gifts nurtured. The need is for an understanding atmosphere in which to discover, experiment and explore with confidence the creative ideas that may eventually free him as an individual.

*　　*　　*

In 1961 I expressed my views on the place of dance programmes in schools and colleges in a paper "The Role of Dance in Education". It was part of a lecture-demonstration which I gave in American Modern Dance techniques and Dance Composition at the National Fitness Centre at Narrabeen, (N.S.W.), Australia.

"We must have a fully developed dance program in education with trained teachers if the children of the next generation are to become dance literate adults."

If dance is to enjoy a better universality in this country, it needs to become more widespread educationally.

Not everyone can avail himself of studio training, nor is every child interested to reach the professional goals of dance—i.e. dance as a career—the way dance can reach everyone so that they have an equal opportunity to discover the life of the dance is through the schools at every level—then through the educational programmes of the Colleges and Universities—a concern for the dance experience in either educational or performing areas in terms of educating the individual as a whole; as a discipline; as a means of communication; as an area of human experience; in the area of creative work and research; the preparation of a knowledgeable and appreciative and informed dance audience; dance educated critics.

This book has grown out of a series of creative ideas, experiments and inventions during the years that I taught modern dance at Fort Street Girls' High School[4] and then at Fort Street High School.[5]

4 1963–1974 at Fort Street Girls' High School, Observatory Hill.

5 1975 at Fort Street High School, Petersham.

The thematic material, questions, and descriptions, presented by myself and the students are a sample of one way to present this type of creative work in education.

The themes are illustrative of some of our workings in the creative process; sometimes a relatively simple approach to an idea and then an increased complexity of resources and application as classes became more aware and knowledgeable in movement vocabulary and developed creative confidence.

The thematic material and its manipulation which is described and annotated during this period of growth and development is chosen for its variety of ideas and creative responses. This segment of work covering a decade of working creatively in dance in education could perhaps be used in creative dance work for infants and primary school children if the way of working was altered to suit the age groups and the capacity of the children's ability. Yet again, one may find sparks of inspiration in the text for drama in education. Many of the creative insights contained in the material could be retained for shaping the creative individuality of the dance student in the studio.

But primarily this creative output is for secondary school students and taught as a specialist creative subject within the Physical Education Department, or as one of the many activities of physical education.

It is too, for student teachers, primary school teachers and lecturers in dance in education who find our methods and concepts useful and stimulating. They may infuse their own material with a new twist, skilfully blending their approach with the essence of the creative purpose—the discovery of unknown and new ways of creative expression.

Create the opportunity for the child to find a direct expression of the personality through the individual and group experience with beauty of movement. Introduce the materials of dance explorations in a situation which will lead to creative action. Create a sympathetic yet challenging environment for the creative process to function thereby becoming articulate in the communication of feelings, thoughts and actions. Discover the latent powers of creative expression and discover the child's capacity for personal artistic growth.

My teaching experiences in the schools in 1962 prior to my appointment at Fort Street Girls' High School could hardly have begun in less auspicious circumstances. I was initiated into the drawbacks, largely of a practical nature that those who undertake to introduce this subject might have to face.

Working areas were often stony and rough or of hot asphalt, and even grassy areas were prickly and uncomfortable in bare feet—and a patch of shade was a welcome shelter on a summer day.

In spite of these somewhat onerous circumstances, classes did experience some improvisation and movement discovery, but because of the short time that I spent in these teaching situations in 1962, I think that the young student would have lost the connection with the creative purpose—unless there was to be some continuation of an educational aim in future teaching of a dance programme.

On my permanent appointment to Fort Street Girls' High School in 1963, I was able to start on my task of building a dance programme (functioning within the Physical Education Department), where *every* young school student would have an opportunity to dance. The majority of the school students had never experienced dance before and few, in fact, knew of its existence in a culturally educated situation. I had to find my way to introduce it so that it would become accepted by the majority of students.

After being involved for the major part of my life in the modern dance as a performer and choreographer and teaching in a studio environment, the introduction of this subject presented certain problems. There were solutions to find and quests to pursue! In my own mind I had to define the goals of professional dance, studio dance and dance in education.

At times it seemed as if the validity of every movement, gesture and step that I made was questioned. I had to find a way of leading the pupils through to the dance by exploration and experiment, and at the same time make the lessons interesting enough to them to ask the *why* of movement. To understand and apply the laws of movement governing the body as an instrument of expression. Allied to this was my belief in the elements, qualities and characteristics of the dance which as I have mentioned earlier in this text, justifies its place in the education of the individual. As regards instruction, one had to tackle this according to the level and capacity of each individual in the class, then set up a programme of work that would encompass the total capacity of the class. This depended on their physical and creative potential and involvement with the dance experience.

Each student had one and sometimes two weekly dance lessons during the six years of her secondary school education, from year seven to year twelve, (with ages ranging approximately from eleven to eighteen years of age). Unlike the early beginnings when the younger students from year seven and year eight (eleven and twelve years of age) were more receptive to the work, the strength of the dance movement then progressed to the senior classes.

The levels of dance efficiency ranged from elementary to advanced. There were always shifts and changes among the classes and individuals concerning growth and development, awareness, responsiveness, concentration, disciplined application, involvement in physical and creative skills.

The programme for creative and artistic growth in dance for all students consisted of:

1. Modern dance technique and its application as a known language of movement.
2. Exploration of new ways of moving.
3. Creative experiences and expressiveness.

This book describes the use of thematic material as one way of working imaginatively within the areas of exploration and creative experiences and expressiveness, and how we built and developed our ideas from a creative standpoint.

Time and space were always set aside for extra sessions for practice and rehearsals for the dance minded students—i.e. (Dance Club). A time for those who wished to extend their range and standard of movement. To work on line, quality and feeling about a movement—to study the complexities of dance. A

9

time to develop their creative and expressive tendencies and work freely on their creative projects, improvisations, or gain insight and experience in composing for dance. A time for us to meet the dance group and choreograph and rehearse for performance. A time for some of the dance students to patiently and tirelessly teach elementary dance technique and improvisation to some of the younger pupils.

If dance technique is taught then it should only serve as a means to an end.

It was quite natural for me to introduce movements that would develop the instrument—the body. Having been educated in the modern dance to move and value my own body and movement image, I tried to enhance the dance capacity of the youngsters by involving them in a system of training the body. To teach them how to develop a flexible body and move with greater ease and co-ordination, to become fluent in bodily movements and movement sequences. To realise the limitation that the anatomical structure might impose and then to overcome this by correcting certain faults and weaknesses in the body structure—to increase the movement potential of the child and sharpen the image of the body. I concentrated on this development with classes by not only introducing technique but by introducing the concept of exploring movement possibilities. I allowed the classes freedom to move in any way they chose—to move differently—to take risks in movement—to make mistakes—to develop a concept about their own bodies and become aware of how they felt about certain movements. To experiment with rhythms, to dance through space, to strive for confidence, to move through levels and to experience time by travelling faster and slower; the precarious balance; the pulls of gravity and the feeling of weight; the power of energy and the different results of releasing the energy—the discovery of the falls—movement discovery.

Too much accent on technique seems to restrict and hamper and I found that sterility of ideas can result. The child can develop a state of reliance on the teacher and may show little inclination to discover and explore and experiment and a reluctance to reach outwards in search of fresh ideas. If teachers insist on introducing technique then they must make sure they are fully cognisant with the teaching points. Analysis of movement techniques needs to be clear and inspiring with a sense of life and musicality—technique needs to be taught as part of the TOTAL concept of dance.

Too much strain produces in some pupils dissatisfaction and little individual creativity results.

I like what Anaïs Nin has to say about the source of creation. "Too great an emphasis on technique arrests naturalness. The material from which I will create comes from living from the personality, from experience, adventures, voyages. This natural flow of riches comes first. The technique is merely a way to organise the flow, to chisel, shape; but without the original flow from deep inner riches of material, everything withers."[6]

As soon as possible move away from systematic and directed ways of teaching and focus the attention of the classes on originality of movement.

Change, renew and redirect the energies of the students towards the exploration of movement and the liberation of the imagination and the freeing of the creative impulses. Through creative tasks each girl discovers her own range of

6 *The Journals of Anaïs Nin*—volume four—Edited by Gunther Stuhlmann. Quartet Books, London.

movement. This way of working decreases self-consciousness and inhibitions and helps to get rid of the fear of moving which constantly interferes with expressive movement and the creative output.

One must be sympathetic in teaching; encouraging the students' creative gifts and receiving what the student has to offer with a spirit of patience and enthusiasm, generous acceptance and appreciation. This way one can help to free the individual to move, guiding the release of imagination through movement and prevent the attempts and results from being sterile. Whatever the creative task, the experiments in shape and form need to be the result of a genuine expressive effort by the students not only with their minds but with their senses and hearts.

There must be a sympathetic atmosphere between the teacher and students —of giving and receiving. It is extremely important as a teacher to constantly develop your creative resources in the classes; generate an excitement of ideas; sounds, movements, shapes, new direction; create images; a new stimulus; be constantly involved in the creative activities of your class; a new awareness of the space and an awareness of relationships. In this way you can regenerate your own and the students' creative activities attuning everyone in the environment to the ideas, feelings, emotions, movements, appearances and associations that play a part in the volume of creative productivity, communicable to you and the creatively responsive groups of students.

Live accompaniment in the form of a pianist was just not available in the schools for teaching purposes and unfortunately I had to use recorded music. In my opinion recorded music is both limiting and restricting. At the very moment when I might want to expand an idea or make a rhythm change, I have had to curtail the structure of a phrase, because of the lack of a live musician to provide the necessary musical stimulus to help what I wanted to say, take place.

I tried using excerpts from a classical music repertoire. Most of the works were not suitable because of *rubato* changes in rhythm and the original theme would be followed by a variation. The musical passages did not remain consistent in rhythm or phrasing to suit the combinations of dance movement or development of creative material.

My own choreography was quite a different matter being able to select musical compositions which were excellent for my ideas and suitable for performance. Some of the compositions used by the dance group were by, for instance, Holst, Debussy, Cowell, Hovhaness, Chavez, Crumb and Stockhausen. The ideal accompaniment is to have the musical score specially written for the dance composition.

It is now possible to obtain recorded piano music by composers who are trained in writing for modern dance techniques, composition and improvisation. This music, by mainly American and English composers, has imagination and continuity. These are enjoyable, expressive and valuable contributions to the lessons and to the dance studies of the students.

I have also experimented with percussion, sounds and silence and verbal imagery as possible sources of accompaniment. Silence was extremely eloquent for the creative material; one can concentrate on the imaginative elaborations of movements and their design, the rhythmic modifications, grouping relationships, the time patterns, over-all shape and emotional intensity of content.

"Verbal imagery" or "word landscapes' was developed out of sheer necessity —out of the search to find new and varied means of accompaniment. I have always liked words; the vital, living, expressive qualities of language. It served as a springboard for the movement and the rhythm, texture and shape of the action. A kind of interplay arose evoking the emotions along with the physical action of movement.

A further source of enlightenment on the dance has been the collection of dance memoranda.

1. Students have designed their own dance collections—photographs, articles, essays, posters and creative projects on dance and the related arts. Over the years I have been the recipient of their many poems, paintings and drawings inspired by the dance, and which have influenced their own creative experiments.

2. Topical pictures gathered from newspapers have illustrated to us elements of composition and linking them with reality, they have finally become stylised into dance movement. A figure crouched desolate with grief has become a line curving inward; the structure of a flower—a study in rhythm; design and dynamics are revealed in the release of energy and shape of movement depicted by athletes in action. Films, books and performances have broadened their general dance education.

3. Notebooks have been kept by the school students on what they see of interest around them—descriptions of people, objects, surroundings, nature, events. I suppose this is what my teacher of choreography[7] meant when she pointed out to me the sculptured figures poised on the crenellations of church buildings—"There is always something to dance about".

I would like to make a few comments about the teachings of dance to males in the school situation. I was aware of the deficiency in this area of teaching when I went to Fort Street High School in 1975 (co-educational).

I had great assistance from the girls whom of course I had taught previously. The valiant efforts of Jeannie supported at times by Julie, introduced the dance to George, one of the male students who was visionary enough to gravitate to this form of movement.

He was one of the most promising athletes in the school and came to dance with a strong, agile movement. A few courageous males joined my special class when they saw the example of the progress achieved by George.

Dance needs to be accepted in the school programme and lessons timetabled (it would probably be taught within the Physical Education Department) with male and female dance-trained instructors. There needs to be more dance at

7 Doris Humphrey (U.S.A.).

college level and economic security for dancers if it is going to progress as a profession.

Once young men experience the movement of dance, they soon come to realise that all the skills they use in sports—muscular control, courage, flexibility, agility, acceleration, elevation, balance etc. are encompassed in the action of the dance vocabulary and techniques of training, as well as qualities of creativity, expressiveness and the extension of personality. They thus become more physically and emotionally fulfilled individuals.

Therefore it was not without struggle that I began the work in an atmosphere that was not oriented towards the culture of dance.

Much of my dance material, technical and compositional, was for trainee dancers and for performance level and seemed little use to youngsters in a school situation. Much of that vocabulary had to be reinvestigated, changed, adapted and selected, reshaped and recreated. It had to be presented in such a way that it would stimulate and motivate the students and still be enjoyable. I had to find a way to make the classes respond and want to *dance*!

I wanted dance recognised to be equal to the other art forms and subjects studied by the pupils at all levels of their education—at the high school level from year seven to year twelve.[8] Slowly I had to replace attitudes of apathy and hostility with interest and enthusiasm. Misconceptions existed in the minds of the students about the meaning of dance and its place in education. Working in bare feet[9] was strange to most of the classes at first and they had to understand the reason for this. They needed to be informed about the history and development of the modern dance—about the use of the bare foot as a pre-requisite for the modern dance vocabulary—realising its difference from other forms of dance and aware also how humanity is expressed through this particular art form. I sought to give the thoughts and expressions of fantasy—as they return to reality—a purpose, an emotion, a feeling. The word-pictures, which are moulded into creative dance forms in the shape of movement pictures are not only a personal affirmation of one's imaginative powers, but need to convey a concern and appeal for one's fellow man.

Each time that the year eight classes (twelve to thirteen years of age) met, the lessons started with a discussion about the style of movement that would be expressive of the different poetic images. The group of children who chose to dance the Poem, "The Sea" invented circular and successive body movements and chose floor designs that would heighten the free flowing undulating movements. Their movement patterns built up to a crescendo through a change of level from low to high and a movement range that increased in rhythm and dynamics. They evolved a directional plan with groups advancing and receding. Movements were successive, curling and uncurling, one movement after the other, fluid and active, then a change of a focal point as the group moved into a circular design with a constant shifting of places and positions. Pulled to the floor, bodies spiralled into a fall, then rose into an upright position with a

---

8 For example, painting, sculpture, pottery, screen printing, poetry, creative writing. Works studied are by such authors as D. H. Lawrence, Tennessee Williams, Albert Camus, Jean Anouilh, T. S. Eliot. Dance works are never studied!

9 The bare foot is significant in the sense that it is the symbol of a dance that revolted against the conformity and rigidity of the Victorian Age. The foot is free, has a close affinity with the earth. It is trained to become as articulate and sensitive as the hand.

backward curve of the body. Finally the tempo changed, and the group altered their direction and pattern, moving into one central point to express a whirl-pool—a visual organisation of continuous movement.

1 A Descriptive Statement—The Theme

The descriptions of the thematic material in this book are illustrated with the kind of verbal activity which I introduce and encourage in my lessons. Generally speaking, preparation and practical work on a theme is just as intense with juniors as it is with senior students. In a creative lesson I spend some part of the time discussing the topic, then the rest of the lesson is spent on practical work. In some of our creative discussions about our ideas, reactions of the students are quite simple and brief but with classes of a more advanced standard I expect more perceptive responses.

One uses a great deal of energy in inducing the minds in the class to become receptive to the creative process. One must stir the sensitivity and inquisitiveness of the group by the use of images, extending the mental representation with quality and meaning. The choice of language in the description of the thematic material should be poetic and lucid, expressive about facts or fantasy, whether the theme is plain or elaborate, simple or extravagant, grotesque, comic or tragic, and whether it is concerned with nature or human beings. One must phrase the questions about the subject matter in a stimulating way; to generate creative thinking and an interchange of concepts which will later be translated into creative movement.

One must be able to determine the value of the contributions in whatever media the students choose as an extension of their ideas. Exchange of ideas can be distinctly inspiring, with a prudent manipulation of the divergent points of view, however haphazard these viewpoints may appear to be.

One becomes resourceful in coping with the stimulation of a multiplicity of impressions (from thirty to forty members of a class) and quick too, in organising the thematic material into a coherent pattern so that one can progress towards a logical development of that theme.

The next stage is a discussion between the class and instructor about the means by which this thematic material can be presented in an aesthetically pleasing dance form. There are decisions to be made about whether the creative effort will be largely individual or consisting of a number of small groups. Whether the form should evolve through improvisation or as a carefully planned structure in the shape of a composition. The groups may wish to make effects with a whole skein of ideas drawn from poetry with movement, invent with fabric or props, or accompany their work with music, thus creating the atmosphere or feeling that they wish to convey. Interchange of ideas and suggestions usually follow about the kind of movements, relationships and the use of space which certain individuals in the class believe would indicate the range and main characteristics of the theme. Naturally there are different reactions to the theme and the way it should be conceived in movement. Some class members tend to stick to conventional attitudes and want to use the movements and spatial designs that they know—while others react against this and are inspired to approach the solution of the particular creative problem with enquiry and search, wanting to produce something that in visual terms is different and new.

No matter how different and varied are the ways chosen to handle the thematic movement material with its contrasting qualities and designs, the value of the creative experiment lies in the growth of the human being as she struggles to find a way of expressing herself.

The vitality of the class then needs to be propelled into the final stages of the creative development. This is the moment when their minds are jolted into awareness and wonder and when they have the freedom and variety to extend themselves into finding an effective form for their ideas, with some originality. The class disperses onto the floor into a space to pursue their independent lines of development. The space is alive with dance students working on the shape of their material. Floor patterns and movement design change constantly until the students feel that they have achieved a relation with the subject matter. Out of dynamics and rhythms of movement spring a sense of energy and a new complexity of rhythms which heighten the interest of a movement.

The harmony of these projects depends on one's total involvement with the class and a concern with the individual dance interpretations of the idea. This sense of harmony will depend on how much of yourself you give to the students, and how much they in turn give of their own selves to a movement. The harmony will be rewarded by students developing as creative persons making a genuine creative effort that is sincerely meant.

As segment by segment of the creative design is constructed I usually go to the different groups and observe their creative workings. I advise, guide, change or re-deisgn if I am asked to do so; "perhaps more proportionate use of space; contrast in movements; directional change; a more linear aspect in the design; bold and large shapes; devices that can add to the impact of the meaning. Capture the intangibles; the pliant mystery of a mood". The groups learn to select or discard movements; to bridge the gap between the meaning and the creative form. They learn creatively if there is an emotional significance in the subject involved; then the groups experiment with lines and expressive elements of dynamics or tensions between figures. All this creative working naturally extends over a period of many lessons when the overall shape often changes and some of the dance students discover new directions or enlarge upon a variation. I often work with one of the groups, listen to them talk about the kind of design they want, or the type of quality of movement needed from a gesture. On completion of the creative conception of the theme, I then spend more time on the final stage of the work.

One-examines the creative effort in terms of the overall design; suitability of movement; choice of music or props (if any); originality of movement; the feeling, mood or atmosphere that the work might evoke. This critical appraisal takes time but it establishes an environment where the students can look at their own work and at the works of others and learn to assess them objectively. I encourage the classes to be selective and discriminating in their opinions—to look at each creative work with insight and to be able to appreciate a genuine creative effort. This creative approach can develop later into a compositional form uniting creative thought with action in the more formal manipulation of the elements of composition. These early creative experiences assist the student in discovering in themselves creative resources and a critical perception and evaluation of the aesthetic. We usually sit in an informal group to introduce a theme or topic or subject. The classes react differently. Some may be slow to accept a theme or interest could be rapid—with others the reactions vary and waver. If one tries to dominate the creative scene the individuals tend to conceal their ideas. It is impossible to predict the level of interest and creative reactions and responses to a theme. Encouragement and opportunity must be given to allow the spirit of enquiry and free flow of imaginative ideas to circulate among the class, as they are all equal contributors in the investigation of the task. It is impossible for me to record the variety of expressive opinions that race through a class. The material can be inspired by realistic concepts or abstract, non-concrete ideas.

At times we could complete a theme in one lesson or it might take weeks of working and reworking before a creative solution is reached that would be acceptable to all of us.   . .

The teacher needs to assume responsibility for the balance and symmetry of the creative growth of the class. To ascertain whether the subject matter can be handled by the groups, watching for problems that may arise and artistically solving them with the students—stimulating curiosity, originality, spontaneity, flexibility and initiative in working creatively. Themes can be suggested by any member of the class. Look for a new way of saying something. One must remember that the thematic movement material will eventually develop into dances.

One Example of THE STARTING POINT FOR A THEME

The colour, shape, texture and movement centred around plant life can be a source of ideas visualised in terms of physical movement—every child will interpret in her own way. Record the movements of flowers and the patterns of leaves and branches—the rhythmic clusters of light and shade. Study the structure of growing things—the interpretation of plant life.

Is the space enclosed or is it expansive—opening out—a tight area—circular or radiating outwards from the centre? Are lines thrown out in a linear projection? Expanding or contracting? Is the design stretched and tall or hanging—(as in the weeping variety of trees)—twisting and turning (as in the curling willow)?

Light or heavy in appearance. Surfaces—connected, flowing, uneven, disjointed, sticky, lumpy, cold, warm, smooth, tough, fragile. Colours—muted, translucent, brilliant, opalescent.

From one of our creative experiences in seeing things around us on Observatory Hill, we produced a piece of creative work. The roots of the giant Moreton

Ascent
Photography: Douglas Thompson

Bay Fig Trees had risen above the ground. They were so large and rough, with deep, gnarled, indentations—creating an appearance of figures twisted in tortuous shapes. One of the students devised a study about Andromeda—the figure in Greek mythology who was chained to the rock and later rescued by Perseus.

The integration of the bare contours of tree forms and the sculptural human shapes, in pulling, resisting, writhing, hanging, twisting and falling movements with the emotional implication of being chained, reflected dramatic visual interest, and originality of the idea.

We have used our own method of approach in the way in which we have interpreted the themes. Should you wish to develop your own imagination and confidence in what you want to say and how you want to express your ideas then try to evolve your own distinctive approach. "Those teachers who from first to last have the task of caring and feeding creativity in young minds"[10] help the individual to discover themselves as a person. As you draw out from the child what he or she is capable of giving you will find yourself becoming concerned with motivation, stimulation, drive, curiosity, hard work, tenacity, conviction; all requirements for creative achievements.

I have often been asked "what led you to the dance?" As a school pupil, I saw a performance by the Bodenwieser Dance Group. They visited our school[11] to perform for the students. This was part of our cultural education to acquaint us with the performing arts. This inspiring group made such an impact on me that I was determined to study if ever the opportunity presented itself and to my great joy, eventually I was able to do so.

I hope that our approach to the creative endeavour outlined here, which has been so enlivening to us at Fort Street Girls' High School, during our times of working together, will stimulate those who are concerned with providing an environment in the classroom for our future painters, writers, dramatists, poets, dancers, inventors and scientists, setting up an even more independent and unique approach to "making-up".

10 New York University Alumni News.

11 The school was S.C.E.G.G.S., Darlinghurst, Sydney.

2 Elementary Creative Techniques

A short discussion in the class about Creativity should precede the lessons for the first few weeks.

"What is Creativity?"

"Have you ever created anything?"

"Do you make things—if so in what medium?"

"Do you use your imagination, or make things with your hands; do you use words, or materials—clay, wire, string?"

"Are you interested in nature—do you ever watch an ant, or butterfly or leaf?"

Respect the confidence of each child as she or he expresses ideas, opinions and feelings about creativity and point out that now we are going to work in another area of creativity in which our medium will be movement and our instrument the body, and our materials will be design, dynamics, rhythm, and gesture.

What is Creativity and What Does it Mean to Me?

Opinions expressed by year seven schoolgirls at Fort Street Girls' High School, average age twelve.

Susan

"Creativity is something made up by your mind. Design and inventions are all part of creations."

Margaret

"Creativity means a considerable amount to me as I have an interest in art and designing. I love doing art with the brightest colours and strangest shapes."

Susanne

"To create is to make things with your hands or imagination like making patterns with shells. A dream is creating something. Creating can be anything you make up yourself."

Camille

"To create is to concentrate on something by closing your eyes and expressing what you feel."

Lynne

"Creativity means to me to be able to let yourself go and use your imagination, for instance as a 'witch' or a 'seaweed floating in water'."

Kay

"You must have ideas and feelings."

Elizabeth

"Dancers create dances. Creativity comes from the soul. You can't really see it at first, it just emerges."

Joan

"Creativity doesn't really mean anything to me because I haven't really time to create anything."

Poppy

"Creativity is a wonderful thing. You can shut your eyes and think of something that you like and try to be it or design it on mud or sand. Many times the design might be hard to draw but it would be fun trying to be it. Creativity is not a set subject but it's your own imagination."

In creativity you can use your thoughts and imagination and create a dance, a mime, a design or a model of your own pleasure. If you like a dance which you have learnt, but don't like the position of the arms and legs, you can create a position of your own. By doing this you could make the dance feel alive and make it feel as if every part of your body is involved in the dance.

3 Creative Experiences

Seeing Things Around Us

Once, we decided to look outside the gymnasium and see the variety of architecture—Colonial, Victorian, Conventional; and the Contemporary glass-walled buildings of our time.

May I suggest that you begin your class with a discussion of shapes around you; oval, rectangular, square, pyramidal, cylindrical, and how these shapes in the skyline affect our scenery and scenes—be aware of how differently each one of us reacts to our surroundings.

More awareness! of structures, textures and materials; of styles of architecture; of the living environment; a search for growing things; colour, shape, and form of human, animal and plant life.

Intensify learning, feeling and enjoyment of the world we live in.

Judith's Group—*Average age 12 years*—*Year Seven*

"The buildings seem to express a child's creation made from building blocks. The domes of the Observatory give the impression of buildings seen in the future.

The twisted and gnarled branches of the tree create the feeling of Andromeda chained to the rock. The roots of the trees look like giant claws reaching out towards one."

Wendy's Group

"I see wide wires that look like string expanding in different directions. Interruption by factory stacks.

I see cars going towards a huge bulge (Sydney Harbour Bridge). This bulge swallows them and they never return. I see millions of coloured squares which remind me of patterns that we draw, but they turn out to be roofs of houses.

There is a tree extending to the sky and it has twisting stems that look like snakes."

Marilyn's Group

"The I.B.M. Building looks like a Japanese house.

There is a yellow dahlia opening like a ballerina in the dance.

Signs jutting out like coat hangers.

I see a ship which looks like a great white giant on a calm green sea—ferry boats are gliding silently."

Jeanette's Group

"A crane; like a daddy-longlegs reaching over its prey. Ants on the ground remind me of rolling beads.

A new building just going up looks as if it is made from matches. The Observatory looks like eggs in egg cups. An unfinished building looks like a honeycomb. The school is a sea serpent appearing on land to die. The wall without windows or doors is frightening. It has·no face. The I.B.M. building reminds me of a curious madman. The rusty steel fence blocks us from the outer world."

*   *   *

We did not confine these creative experiences to observation of architecture, but to many scenes in the area. We observed the skyline, contours of the terrain, hills, steps, slopes of grassy areas, windows, roof-tops, doorways. The shape and rhythms of the street—people walking or standing idle, in conversation, at work. An accident—converging to the focal point, excitement, discord—drama —moods, atmosphere, character, subways, boxes, umbrellas, junk, the wharves.

We record our impressions of what we see around us—the patterns of people and the environment that co-exist.

Extend the creative experience in as many ways as possible—natural and man-made.

All odours—sweet, pungent, evil, unpleasant. The sensation of touch. Heat and cold—colour—sky clouds and sun—weather. All sounds from the dry click of a leaf falling to the metallic whine of a jet plane.

We had many sessions in the space outside; the environment and the land-scape became a source of ideas—we found many starting points for creative movement themes.

Atmosphere, shapes, relationships were woven into movement fantasy during the lessons on the green slopes of "the hill" (Observatory Hill).

Students twisted their bodies into imaginary beings around protruding tree roots. Hollow shapes hid in the corrugations of massive tree trunks.

Find a precipitous slope—run, leap, roll—no obstacles—just free expansive energetic action. Struggle upward to the top of the hill. Twist, crawl, pull yourself along. Walk gently among the long grasses—climb and swing from the trees—watch the movement of the branches. Make flower chains and garland yourself—festoon your wrists, neck, head and ankles. Put a shell on your eye-lid—ferns across your face—weave branches and leaves into a fan— or an umbrella—move into flower shapes.

Go to the sea. Feel the poetry of the water and breezes—create a movement study with sound, rocks and water. Use your body and parts of the body in different ways—imagine that they are your partner—Interpret their texture and form. Relax in a rock pool—move your fingers and toes like a sea creature —whirl across the sand—curl up among the rocks in shell formation.

4 Creative Work and Research

Thematic Material

LIVELY

(From Freda Miller's Record for Dance)

Discuss "Lively": like acids bubbling and effervescing, excitement and joy, quick, light, short-lived—good news, entertainments, clowns, jugglers, acrobats, quaint movements, unbelievableness. Small movements, parallelisms—capriciousness, irregularities.

In a Toy Shop. A Circus. The Zoo Story.

Suggestions by the Class for Group Study of a Toy Shop

Popular Characters

Golliwogs, bears, puppets, fairy dolls, ballerina dolls, rag dolls, Spanish dancers, stuffed animals, mechanical toys. Toy soldiers, Charleston dolls, acrobats.

A monkey playing a drum. A snake charmer and a snake. An animal band. A rocking horse.

In the script for the dance study relate a toyshop situation to life, e.g., ballerina doll falls in love with a toy soldier but he "runs down" and falls to the floor.

A Circus Study would have the same piquant style, capricious and yet fantastic, a sadness lurking behind the gay lively impossible movements.

There is also something of the feeling of the Gailliard in the lively tunes of Freda Miller's Album. According to Louis Horst's lectures on composition in pre-classic forms[12] the themes of good news, holiday, frolic, caprice, laughter, exuberance, heyday, mischief are composed in the style of Gailliard. The characteristics of such would be bouncy, gay, quick, hopping, with rhythmic variety—little jumps, gallop—quick and sudden.

The Zoo Story has a combination of the qualities of the Gailliard and secular Medieval dance study.

Devise a study: Snakes, tree, crocodiles, palings of the enclosure, keeper, tourists, two grown-ups and little boy, variety of animals. Characteristics of

12 Lectures at Summer School of Dance at Connecticut College, New London, Conn., U.S.A., 1958 and 1959.

animals—mimetic movements of monkeys, slither of crocodiles, heavy awkwardness of bears, sinuous twisting of snakes, teasing of boy, elegant display of lyre-bird.

There should be an element of surprise—contrast when boy is snapped at by crocodiles and is eaten!

A Creative Story for Lively

A TOYSHOP COMPOSED BY A GROUP OF YEAR SEVEN GIRLS
SETTING: Toyshop.
MAIN CHARACTERS: Golliwog, rag doll, fairy doll, two wooden soldiers.
SCENE I: Everything is quiet in the shop. The toys look miserable. Suddenly the golliwog springs to life and he starts to move about. He runs over to the rag doll and winds her up. He winds up the fairy doll who sees the wooden soldiers lying stiffly in their boxes. She waves her wand over them.

The soldiers stiffly and disjointedly start to rise and march around the toyshop. All the toys play, the rag doll is lively and is jealous of the beautiful fairy doll who flirts with the toy soldiers.

Gradually they wind down and fall in a heap on the floor.
SAND-GAME, Kerry's interpretation of Lively.

The penguins are gradually strolling up on to the sand and rocks from the water. At first they stroll about and play executing little steps. They roll in the sand and play in groups. There is great excitement. One sees a fish thrown up on to the sand and goes to claim it. Then the penguin is joined by a second and the playful curiosity over the fish turns into a fight. The other penguins join in as they also want part of the fish—there is great movement and a big struggle ensues. As they struggle a huge sea creature approaches and claims them one by one—some struggle to escape, some die of shock and some are eaten by the monster.

MYSTERIOUS

(Suggestion from Freda Miller's Album for Dance)

Let us discuss the connotation of Mysterious.

The dictionary says mysterious is applied to "that which excites curiosity, wonder, but is impossible or difficult to explain or solve. That is inscrutable which is completely mysterious and is altogether incapable of being searched out. A novel, a story, or a play involving an event—anything or everything that remains so secret or obscure as to excite curiosity."

The word mysterious has as its noun mystery and can be applied to secret rites and religious doctrines.

Class definition from year seven
"Mysterious is something that is hard to understand—secretive." "It makes you feel creepy." "It is like a mist creeping slowly over you."
"Do you like mystery?"
"Yes because it excites me."

26

"When night comes I feel that there are mysterious happenings."

"Mysterious reminds me of strange paintings—and colours that have secrets."

"Night is mysterious because it is dark and there are sounds which you sometimes can't recognise. Sometimes I am frightened."

"What colours are mysterious?"

"Murky colours—dirty colours."

"Blackish browns." "Greenish greys." "Dark purple."

"Strange blacks and even pale grey-white."

"Trees look ghostly and mysterious at night."

"Sometimes women look mysterious if they have painted faces and you see them under a street light."

"The cat is a mysterious creature."

What kind of movements will you make?

"Weak movements." "Slinky and creepy movements."

"We will not move a great deal."

"We might make twisted and tortured and strange designs."

"A seething mass of shapes."

The children will consciously subject themselves to their idea of mysterious —they will fiercely express their interpretation and their study should take on strange overtones which will be reflected in their shapes. There will be discord in their work and all their movements will be dissonant—an unharmonious movement or combination of movements.

*   *   *

IMAGE

I have asked for an image, a picture of something that has meaning for the pupils; to present their idea in words, and then to extend the image pattern into paint. When the poem and painting are reviewed and we know what the poem is arriving at then alter its medium and translate the image into movement.

The poetic imagination can be translated into the dance through the language of movement—the child must be sympathetic with the images and develop a state of mind when she is capable of seeing "the uncertainties, mysteries, doubts without any irritable reaching after fact and reason".[13]

In her poem "The Sea" Susan expressed the savagery of the sea and illustrated its feeling of power in a painting of dark blue and sombre greyish white abstraction:

13 *The Poetic Image* by C. Day Lewis, published by Jonathan Cape 1947, p. 67.

A hungry monster crashing on sand,
Devouring ships and men;
Demanding the fear of all that lives,
On water, air or land.
The monster roars and swirls and breaks,
And threatens all things alike;
For it is the ruler of all our lives;
And leaves disaster in its wake.

In "Faces of Fear" Helen represented her desolate and bleak images by a painting in greys, white, red and black. A strange shape, it resembled a primitive mask, groteque, weird, and with a hint of loneliness in its expression:

What is fear?
Fear is the yearly examination
Fear is the monsters in a young
Child's bedroom at night.
Fear is being blind and without sight.
Fear is not being loved.
Fear is a negro in America.
Fear is not being wanted.
Fear is being alone when your heart
Is troubled and the black pools of
Night wait to swallow you up.
Fear is death and not having flowers
From loved ones on your grave.

A kind of freakish gaiety echoed through the colourful movement combinations in "The Sparks"—pinks and orange, greens and blue.

The Sparks
Lynn—12 years
O artist of the greatest degree,
Draw your finest picture for me,
Make it move, make it dance,
Let the world be entranced,
Up it goes and down it comes,
Moving sidewards, shaping shadows
Tell your story let it live to its glory
Then when your tale has been told
Bid you fade away to die.

The type of dance material selected for "The Sparks" was based on variations of the run, leap and jump using acceleration and staccato to communicate expectant and arresting aliveness. Lively clapping and stamping suggested a joyous, carnival-like atmosphere. The insistent rhythms by feet and hands were strong and precise. This rhythmic movement phrase recurred at certain intervals after the introduction of other lively and spontaneous movement, as in a rondo form.

The texture of this dance study was sharp and broken, a geometric abstraction of angular shapes, all parts moving in a synthesis of angles and lines to the accompaniment of tactile and vocal sounds to stress fragmentation—and nervous tension.

Masks enhanced the subject matter of Helen's poem "Faces of Fear". The students made fantastic mask-shapes of reds and blues so that the effects were sombre and tortured. Some wanted to hide their identity completely—they did this by draping themselves with material—to give a haunting mysterious dignity to their movements. The movement line and quality was in twisted and distorted combinations of taut angles of bodily movements and overall shapes to give emotional distortion, brutality, and fear.

A LEAF

FLIES

FLOATS

SCATTERS

A LEAF　　　TWISTS

FALLS.

Impressionistic "Leaves" was a collection of real leaves in different shapes and colour patterns.

From the beginning of one image or word picture, several poetic images emerged. There were dark and light images and we had to find the natural creative relationship between them and imaginative movement. The child's mind needs to be free to awaken the fears and fantasies of the dream world— probing the creative imagination and so capturing the images and projecting it into dance movement.

WORDS

I often introduce "words" to my students as another means of encouraging them to create. This helps to break down the aura of mystery that surrounds the creative effort, and keeps the class interested to develop skills and co-ordination, which will lead to more effective performance. Rarely do I include more than three or four "words" in the lesson—the students also select "words" and we attempt to generate as much receptivity to the material as possible. For instance—the number of "words" used in a lesson, the degree of difficulty, when to introduce the relationship between "words" and movement and the best age to start the students can be decided by the teacher. This is a very flexible project and the class and myself found it quite rewarding achieving so much movement in such a short time.

Spire: Response—lofty expresses deep, religious feeling, pointing heaven-ward, a cutting edge, sharp point. In terms of movement, the action is elongated, needle-like measured. Slow or quick, and sharp in dynamics—an arrow-like precision.

Vertical—some positions were either on both feet or on one leg, and taken either standing stretched up or from kneeling positions. Some lay on their backs and directed the vertical line through an arm or leg extension. The rhythm was unbroken. A straight line.

Glass eye: Response—cold, unseeing. The eye of Cyclops, sightless pits of gloom, transparencies, secret societies, rites, searching.

In Terms of Movement: Angular, strange design, a feeling of distortion, lines can be two dimensional. Arms and legs in geometric shapes. Discover different parts of the body that can take the weight; slow and even rhythm; an awkwardness of the feet and legs—deliberate shaping of the body. Intro-spective, the feeling of the shapes pulling back into oneself. Nothing robust or symmetrical, or expansive.

Silver Pellets: Response—shining, metallic, blinding, stinging, sharp and hard, unyielding, hail-stones, whip-like, incongruities, nettles, jibes, miseries.

In Terms of Movement: Instantaneous in all directions, rapid changes of movement and direction and levels—the unexpected, agitation, thrusts into the air and to the floor. Sudden changes. Broken and accented rhythms. Different parts of the body become the focus for a penetrating beat or dynamic contraction. The body is jerked into the air, sideways, forwards, backwards and to the floor. The figures are pursued by flying objects, jagged metal.—They run in all directions.

War: Response—I read a passage from Selected Documents.[14] This is in the form of a letter describing a young boy's feelings about the war in Poland. Terror, suffering, pitiful, battleground, hate, noise, protest, blood—Goya's savage commentary on the horrors of war. We studied Guernica[15] and saw the barbaric symbols and heroic struggles in the design.

In Terms of Movement: Forceful rhythms. Movement was to convey an over-all mood of battle; of ferocity, destruction and exhaustion and an over-flowing sensibility in the suffering and despair of men. As we concentrated on

14 A Modern History Source book, published by McGraw Hill.

15 A painting by Picasso.

Guernica we accentuated distortion and dissonance in every line of the body. Turbulence was depicted by figures thrown against one another in a struggling mass. Thrusts of the outstretched hand; open mouths,[16] distortion in the lines of the head. Groteque savagery in the juxtaposition of group studies suggesting bestiality. Repetitious, strident, movement indicative of the arrogance of war, disciplined and geometric—the inevitability, passionate yet controlled emotion. The dynamic movement should denote tremendous physical exertion as one group breaks through the rigid lines of the group who stand with feet, hands and body ready to repell all opposing forces.

Flowering Branch: Response—cherry-trees, perfume, Persian miniatures, blossoms, honey.

In Terms of Movement: The pattern for flowering branch was created as a group design for three or four figures. The arrangement of the group design was circular or semi-circular or asymmetrical.

There were groups with fanciful designs using only hand movements. The fingers undulated in miniscule and delicate tracery. Most of the groups sat or knelt on the floor so that they could concentrate on the theme. Bodies bent forward and as they arose they opened their arms successively, arching the back as they did so—a harmonious opening and closing, a free-flowing use of line created by the supple body, shoulder, arm, elbow, head and neck movement, and deeply curved in shapes which were somewhat ornamental—reflecting delicacy and refinement of their central flower pattern.

BALLOONS

"BALLOONS BRING JOY"

"THEY ARE UNPREDICTABLE"

"SADNESS AND FEAR WHEN THEY BURST"

"BALLOONS ARE LIGHT—AIRY—WEIGHTLESS—THEY FLOAT"

"FESTIVALS—CLOWNS—CIRCUSES"

"YOU CAN CHANGE THEIR SHAPE"

"A CAPSULE"

"GAIETY"

"FLAMBOYANT AND FREE!"

"SENSE OF LONGING WHEN THE BALLOON FLOATS AWAY AND OUT OF SIGHT"

"BOUNCY AND BUMPY"

"EXCITING COLOURS"

"SUSPENSE AND SURPRISE"

16 "The Cry", a painting by Munch.

I suggest to the class that they find a place on the floor either standing, or sitting or in a lying position and try these simple movements based on the inhalation and exhalation of the breath. The use of the breath rhythm based on my dance experience with Gertrud Bodenwieser and Doris Humphrey was invaluable in achieving through body movement the round, circular and tube-like shapes of balloons and the lively contraction and expansion of these body shapes.

The following definitions on the breath rhythm represent the theories by those pioneers of the modern dance who applied this basic principle to their own philosophy of movement.

Gertrud Bodenwieser stressed the life of the movement through the use of breath—

Opening and closing, lift and drop; her system of dance movement followed the rise and fall of the breath and controlled the unfolding of movement by the body and its parts with its different degrees of withdrawal and renewal of energy, sometimes harmonious or sharp and percussive or gradations of movement from soft and delicate to strong and dramatic. These variations of pulsations in movement and the idea that movements grow out of each other are then subject to the dynamic element which enters into the movements of the modern dance by the increase in the intensity of the movement.

For instance, you can slowly lift the right arm as you breathe in and lower it as you breathe out—long sustained unbroken movements with long continuous in-breaths or out-breaths.

Short sharp staccato movements with breath accents in or out.

The rise and fall of the body can be increased or decreased, depending on the breath intake or output; movements can be isolated to different parts of the body; inverted; broken up into smaller and smaller rhythms; backwaves, forward waves and side waves, with the rippling evenly moving throughout the body; or rippling isolated to the arms and head and chest only; percussive movement of different parts of the body.

Fluttering fingers and curved hands recall the shapely opening of the balloon—hands curve in circles and twist as in a figure of eight—others pulsate through their hand and wrist movements—

"Now, through the breath"—

"Inflate and deflate—rise and fall;"

"Expansion and contraction and relaxation—"

"Breathe in and out"—

"Long breaths in and short breaths out—"

"The life of the movement depends on the use of the breath—"

"Now experiment using the breath rhythm."

32

"Long breaths in and three short sharp breaths out;"

"Now breathe in—in sharp intakes of breath and a long, long, sustained breathing out—"

"As you breathe in or out, change your dance position continually—"

"Let your movement follow the rise and fall of your breath—"

"Let it flow—"

Begin experimenting through the breath with different parts of your body, as you inflate and swell and expand into what finally will be your balloon shape. Then the slow or fast breathing out will release your energy and the movement will change and become compressed.

VARY THE SPEED AND DYNAMICS (soft and strong) of your breath rhythm and your movements will constantly change.

Some of the class begin to move freely and spontaneously in lying, sitting, kneeling or standing positions—

The body or parts of the body begin to change into new and sometimes startling movements produced by this new motivation through the breath rhythm so that there is a new freedom for ideas.

One arm curves to the side, the second arm follows successively; the body bends into a side curve and the leg is just lifted slightly off the floor to complete the half circle.

The upper body rotating with the arms outstretched and slightly curved upwards and the shift of the weight moving through the centre from left to right.

Slim light pencil-jumps (accented from two feet and land on one foot) propel the body in any direction—the effect is one of animation—rubber balls bouncing, the jerky movements of puppets on a string.

Some balance an imaginary balloon on their feet—they toss, roll, kick—

"I am balancing mine on my head." A balloon-like face with cheeks puffed out and the head moving up and down and circling with the feet constantly shifting the weight by moving on the spot with little pattering steps.

Percussive half turns with changes of direction and then a curvilinear balance as the body is poised before a fast percussive contracted fall onto the floor.

Balloons are held, balanced, freed and sometimes caught—all sizes and shapes—some burst and there is the moment of disappointment and crumbling —movements become smaller and smaller.

Then once again the figures go spinning through the space with lightness and speed and colour and vitality.

THE IMAGINARY BALLOON by one member of my class was very appealing.

Starting simply, she blew up her balloon—expanding and expanding until she became the shape with her whole body, arms and face—yet it was an illusive moment and she perched in a balance on the balls of her feet—

Changing weight and reaching upwards into the space you felt the floating movement of the balloon.

And then she joined the chase; racing in leaps and runs across the floor; turning and gliding, dancing with a wild rhythm, pursuing, half-circling, spiralling to the floor and moving through the space again. She released the string—the form of the body crouched—then the fluttering of fragmented movements as she tried to recapture her gaiety.

*   *   *

MUSIC AND MOVEMENT

It is common knowledge that the combination of music and dance helps to create the artistic completeness which then arouses that reaction of aesthetic pleasure when we either watch a piece of work or dance in it ourselves. The synthesis of musical sound and dance appeals most strongly to children and dance students of all ages and should be present from their earliest dance lessons. Word, song, percussion all contribute to the music that can accompany the accents and the rise and fall of movement.

In the introduction, I have said that there is now a large and varied collection of music recorded for the accompaniment of the modern dance.[17] Many of these experienced and talented people have written their compositions in association with dancers and dance educators from studios and dance departments of colleges and universities throughout the U.S.A.—so many original compositions for techniques of different styles, movement sequences, improvisations and specific creative projects.

There are some excellent English recorded compositions for music and movement, and there is now recorded material emerging from Canada and Australia. Through the flow of music for dance from simple combinations to the most complex, there is an assured enrichment for lyrical and dramatic movements, leaps, jumps, falls, rhythmic patterns and gradations of tempo.

So the teacher needs to become familiar with a wide range of music, usually piano pieces but not always; not only thinking of dance in terms of counts, but in feeling, expressive quality and interpretation. Phrasing should be sensitively developed; counts accented and movements extending to the end of the phrase —it is the teacher's own choice of accompaniment which will sustain the interest of the students. Let them listen to it carefully over and over again so that they become perceptive about the piece they intend to relate to movement —so that there is a powerful and energetic and joyous interaction of the two.

It seems very rare to have a live accompanist in a dance in education programme, so for expressive pieces for performance, there is the whole range of the development of music from the earliest times to contemporary develop-

---

17 Composer-pianists, Sarah Malament, Freda Miller, Pia Gilbert, Edward Muller, John Coleman (associated with Hanya Holm), Cameron McCosh (associated with Martha Graham and Mary Anthony), Douglas Nordli (assicated with Bruce King), Evelyn Lohoefer De Boeck.

Spaced out in a circle   *Photography: Kay E. Martin*

General Grouping—Reaching upward
Photography: Kay E. Martin

Point of Contact
Photography: Denise Fletcher

Side Contraction
Photography: E. Waite

ment. Depending on one's idea, theme and motive and thematic development and the effect to be created, so will depend the choice of music.

The students choose music expressive of their themes and as much as possible are guided to mirror the character and spirit of the idea—the dramatic expression of Pictures at an Exhibition by Moussorgsky; the romantic and inspiring Peer Gynt Suite by Greig; the impressive The Planets by Holst; the wizardry of fairy tale and folk song in Baba Yaga and The Enchanted Lake by Liador. The Colour Symphony by Bliss, each movement inspired by the symbolism of a colour—the rhythmic shimmer of Stravinsky in Spring Dance or the brooding atmosphere of The Sacrifice,[18] the expressive fanciful haunting allurements of Ricki Wakeman's compositions or the enchanting Carnival of the Animals by Saint-Saens.

18 From Le Sacre du Printemps (the Rite of Spring) by Stravinsky.

Tension or suspense, lyricism, humour, an atmosphere of violence, explosive bursts of energy, experimentation or expansion, the quality of dynamic development and in the music and dance organism a totality whatever the expressive idiom.

I am especially fond of such composers as Kodaly, Scriabin, Bartok, Poulenc, Satie and Debussy, Respighi, Hindemith and Villa-Lobos, Chavez—or exploring the development of electronic music.

MOON—SEA—CLOUD

While I was preparing the background for the themes Moonlight, Cloudburst and Sea-weed, I felt that we might search further into some reading matter for spontaneous images.

The class and I decided to read some poetic works in the hope that we might find a new direction and deepen our movement approach. Anything to prevent tameness and dullness!

The poet constantly shows up aspects of thought about the human condition, or the phenomenon of nature. He focuses his attention on these thoughts.

By sensitising ourselves to these aspects, we can discover in ourselves another viewpoint. I have tried to encourage this conviction in my students. I believe that one can develop the capacity to tune into the way an artist is expressing himself through his art.

This deepens our own personal thoughts and adds lucidity to our own creative process.

We read a number of Shelley's poems. His language is so lyrical, all grace and symmetry and enriched by purity of form. Their suitability was matchless, especially: A Vision of the Sea; The Sensitive Plant; The Cloud; To the Moon and To the Earth, Mother of All. The poet's description of nature was expressed with such harmony that one's senses were greatly enriched. We took great pleasure in reading these poems and discovered the full impact of lyrical genius which absorbed our curiosity, quickened the intellect and aroused our emotions. The aesthetic pleasure that we experienced from the poetry suited so well the nature of the themes we were about to embark upon. Our focus was more sharply concentrated in this region and we had learned to profit from this fresh insight—to translate this experience into the realm of our own experimentation with movement, and the movement themes that we had chosen to work on.

We, after all then, through a selection of fresh improvisational material had to supply the visual truth in dance, the patterns, shape, rhythms, feelings vital in the fullest expressive sense of the meaning of—Moon—Sea—Cloud—

*   *   *

37

Lyrical Trio
Photograph : Robert Walker

From Lyrical dance piece L'Isle J
Photograph : Robert Walker

Top: **Curve**

Creative project "Moonlight", a combined work between teacher of dance and teacher of music. There is a great potential for ideas with other departments.

If you possess a department of music, drama or art collaborate with the staff and relate your dance activities to theirs. If these departments are at first apathetic to your subject you can create a better understanding and a genuine interest if you show your work to the staff as much as possible. Give suggestions to the teachers on how these subjects can be related.

Suggest projects which can be done in collaboration with the art department. For instance encourage groups of the dance students to paint and draw—put their feelings and ideas about life and design on canvas—taking movement as a topic encourage some to make a sculpture from wire or metals or wood.

Gather as many poems as possible on all the topics that you have used for your improvisational studies. Then interest an art group and inspire them to paint or draw the images. If the class needs guidance in writing poems suggest to the teacher of drama that she assist them in a creative writing lesson.

Much of the rhythmic training for dance can be assisted by the music staff.

The elements of body percussion that are taught in a music class can be followed up in a dance class where percussion is used for accompaniment. There is too little collaboration between school departments—be irrepressible!

Talk about your subject with others and invite them to see your work.

Music visualisation is the translation of the form of a musical composition into movement.

It closely follows the harmony, melody and rhythm of the structure.

The length, strength or weakness of a note or chord is exactly interpreted into movement—in this method the feelings, moods or themes and their variations are expressed in the musical composition and followed by the dancer or dance chorus.

*   *   *

MOONLIGHT—Music: Clair de Lune by Debussy. A study in music visualisation.

Introduce the idea from which a creative project can be built.

Let the class sit in a group around you on the floor. Begin the lesson with a discussion on creativity which will be an extension of a talk given at the beginning of their first dance lesson. You will have to introduce your subject and no matter how much time this takes, experience has shown that the early discussion of dance and creativity is of the utmost importance. This will be a combination of that earlier preparation.

We have found out that children express themselves in different ways. Children express themselves through paint. They draw and sketch. Others make things—they design clothes, collect shells and make jewellery. Some will make sculptured shapes from bottle top shavings, tin cans, wire or wire netting.

Some write poems.

A great feeling of interest and respect should develop from the way in which they seek self-expression.

You can introduce your subject in a new way this time by telling the class that you used to dance.

"I would lock myself in a room or use the whole house if my parents were out and the long hall was especially favoured as it gave lots of space for jumping and leaping. I would then turn on the radio and dance This would develop into a long and exhaustive improvisation—moving for as long as I was able."

Now play the record Clair de Lune, by Debussy—Moonlight—and all sit down and listen. When the record has ended discuss with the class:

1. Ideas and opinions about the music.
2. Does it describe "Moonlight"?
3. What kind of movements would you make?

Can you construct your dance improvisation round an idea—will you be able to carry it through, or will your improvisation be an endless series of unrelated movements?

Respond to the idea by describing how you feel towards moonlight. Share your ideas for the imaginative setting of the theme.

Analyse the music in terms of qualities and if your training in music is limited prepare your musical analysis with the music teacher.

What kind of movements would you make?

Soft, slow, graceful, floating, long, delicate, quick and light, flowing and stretching, continually unfolding full of rise and fall, curved and slightly mysterious. There is opportunity for changing of level and perhaps of projecting your ideas through only one direction as if one was dancing in a shaft of moonlight.

What does moonlight mean to you? Ideas from the class

Leonie: *12 years. Year seven.*

A silvery road, long movements, reaching out for something, perhaps you want to reach the trunk of a tree or the sea and when you reach it, the moonlight spreads and covers you.

Julie: *13 years. Year eight.*

"Identify yourself with the moon. I think that I am the moon, that I cast long shadows—that I shed a yellow light and I see the long black shadows contrasted with the yellow and silvery light. I would move in long gliding steps trailing a long piece of shining material. I am unreachable."

Tara:

"I think it is like a small white flower and then it opens up and there is a light inside—the light shines more brightly as the flower opens and the petals seem to be the rays of moonlight."

Lynden:

"I compare it to a silver cloth. It can add beauty, it can make things ghostly. It makes shadows long and they blow in the sky. It is like a window cut in the sky. It has a cold beauty—like a statue!"

Other descriptions by class members:

Moonlight is peacefulness.
Like a creature coming out of the darkness.
Like a silvery river, twisting, twirling.
Ever wandering, ever whirling.

Let us begin

Find a space on the floor—settle yourself into a position from which your improvisation will grow.

Begin to build your images for moonlight improvisation.

Perhaps your movement will be clear, cold and hard and brittle. Perhaps you will be silvery brightness on the water—or the pale ghostly light in a dark wood.

Perhaps you will suggest the feelings of love and be a soft and clinging moonbeam.

Or will you be lonely—sitting alone in a shaft of light—or will you dance sadness—or be lightness, dancing on forever over the cold, hard sand?

And when you are ready begin, and find the feeling of ecstasy that comes through movement as you listen to this piece of music. The ecstasy of interpreting your ideas of moonlight—the clearness of music, the breathless unreal quality, the racing human passion and then the peace—the feeling of reaching for the intangible as the moon fades into the dark sky.

And when you are ready, begin!

At the end of the improvisation discuss with the class their interpretation. Did the movements convey the meaning of the subject?

Could you translate your ideas into movement?

Were you light and lovely and delicate enough?

Did your moonlight improvisation have any content and did it have a form.

If the drama teacher can be present at this creative dance work then she can begin to relate the drama to the dance, pointing out that although the media are different the result is the same and that the theme of moonlight can now be interpreted through poetry.

Let her suggest to the class that they compose a poem on "Moonlight" using the words as movements, creating a poem which is descriptive, expressive and full of imagery.

42

Julie: *12 years.*

Starlit, moonlight, streaking bold,
Showering to earth in a sheet of gold
Hitting trees then passing round
Pouring down to the dark underground.
It is a wonder on this cold night
To rodents the moon is such a welcome sight,
With the shadows it makes on the dreary walls
As the sorry song of the barn-owl calls.

Helen: *year seven.*

Silvery beams across the floor,
Light on the windows, light on the door.
A blue-grey mist descends from the sky,
From where does it come?
From the moon on High.
And silence spreads everywhere.
Bats and owls flit here and there.

CLOUDBURST

To make each improvisation a completely satisfying experience each theme is improvised spontaneously freeing the child's resources of mind and body, and contributing to the growth of personality by encouraging in the class a genuine freedom for self-expression and originality.

Discussion, exchange of ideas about the kind of movements suitable to the theme, make for a thorough preparation which should result in a rich improvisation.

The movement expression for Cloudburst will be in groups and as it is a dramatic improvisation the class may use sound accompaniment. Approach the improvisation as a shared experience. Questions on the theme must be varied and numerous and highlight the subject.

How will Cloudburst best be presented?

Give me an expressive description of a storm—

What forceful elements can be used as material for the theme?

Is sound a good idea to accompany this improvisation?

Does this theme suggest using group forms?

Suggestions for developing Cloudburst (from Year Seven and Year Eight).

Creative material suggested by the class: "We are molecules—the higher we go up the heavier we become. We pack together in great cloud formations—we are different shapes and forms at different levels".

"Some of us move slowly, some of us scurry and move quickly. We burst and fall then hit the ground like hailstones, bursting and bounding everywhere."

"The dark clouds appear and creep across the sky."

"As the clouds come together they crash, and here you can make crashing sounds."

"The wind springs up and gets stronger and develops into fierce winds which push the rain groups along."

"These rain groups mingle with the other cloud groups and the mass gets bigger and bigger."

"The clouds spread out in different directions."

"We think that there should be lightning flashes—streaks of sharp movement."

"The fierce winds group breaks up the cloud groups into rain and girls are tossed everywhere.

Here the storm should be at the highest point and the sound[19] can be used dramatically as the clouds burst.

"We would like to have some plants that are growing peacefully then are tossed about by the winds and then break to pieces when the clouds burst. They are up-rooted."

"When everything is destroyed can we have stillness and some brightness growing up out of the earth."

After the feverish movement improvisations of the second year classes had ended, then imagination warmed once more to my idea of expressing the theme

"Cloudburst" in poetry.

Before long, I had verses handed in to me; the pupils hopeful that they had caught in words the atmosphere of uneasy excitement that they had shown in their wildly, rhythmic tossing movements of the dance.

> Wash! sh, sh, goes the howling wind,
> Ss's, an evil wind that has sinned.
> Killing helpless things,
> Thinking he's better than other kings.
> Too strong, too strong for birds' wings.
>
> Pit! pat, now the droppy rain falls,
> Blong! blink, onto the ground falls icy balls.
> Rumble! roar, that's what the thunder says.
> Crackle! crack, lightning as stiff as clay.
> What a day, what a day.

Another group, moving in unison with heavy, sluggish, dragging walks and crawls set out to give the feeling that something was about to happen.

---

19 A group using percussion instruments can accompany the improvisation.

The wind rustling through the trees, sounded like
The cry of the angry sea,
I felt a stuffy feeling inside of me.
Gloomy clouds hung overhead
There was a heavy feeling in my tense body,
Of a burden laid upon my neck.

Everything is quiet, dull and dark,
And nothing could be heard but the song of a lark.
    Then suddenly, without warning,
Came a threatening Boom!
A streak of lightning,
And an atmosphere of gloom.

The stamping of bare feet, and the moaning, tossing, twirling circular group
illustrated in movement language the freakish eruptions of a storm.

I am fearless!
I am great!
When I'm around
I'm full of hate.
Teasing! Tanting!
Roaring! Ranting!
Horrifying! Striking!
I am frightening.
There's a victim—
Well, what about that?
See him running—
Off with his hat!
Rumble! Rumble!
Clash! Boom!
Watch people running
See some zoom!
An electric flash
Like a strike of light;
When I am gone—
All will be bright.

SEAWEED

"The anatomical organisation not merely of human beings but of animals, plants, bacteria, crystals, rocks, machines and buildings. The simplicity and complexity of their forms, their articulation, the disposition of stresses and strains in living and non-living structures.

Recognition of the qualities of things; their hardness and softness, heaviness and lightness, tautness and slackness, smoothness and roughness.

Recognition of unities and similarities, rhythms and analogies, differences.

The character of space, the penetration of space.

The nature of illumination; its determination of what we see (as opposed to what we know otherwise than by vision from a static point in space). The news value of colour.

The way our reading of experience is controlled by the means by which we perceive."[20]

Find a place on the floor—lie down and close your eyes.[21]

The important thing is to rest—relax. Just feel yourself becoming limp—let everything loosen—insteps, toes, feet, knees, thighs, buttocks, shoulders, neck, stomach, head, face muscles, fingers—
Now empty your mind and breathe deeply.
Cast your mind now back to the sea—under the ocean—

Imagine you are a tiny seed and you are blown by the wind down into the curling water.
Travel downwards, fall and disappear.

Some were swift in their motion and were buried in the greenish shadows.

OR you perhaps did not travel far; but suddenly sheltered in clear blue water on a sandy floor OR otherwise lay hidden under a brown rocky ledge—feel the shape of your movements changing.

But wherever you alight you will put down your moorings and cling.
What kind of sea-weed will you become?
Will you be that spongy, clinging, sea lettuce, a pale bouquet, shuddering and flattening against rocks.
If you are round and small, smoothly strung together—nodding as the current gently swirls you to and fro—you will become Neptune's necklace—adorning—bobbing—
Mustard and golden green-brown, slanting and jagged—rough harsh coraline.

As you grow you will feel the water swirling around you—you will feel your texture—you will become stronger, more feathery or slender, tough or spiky—harsh and cruel, soft and delicate.

20 Herbert Read—*A Concise History of Modern Sculpture*, p. 215, Thames and Hudson.

21 The development of "Seaweed" as a creative dance form is based upon the idea and method of teaching devised by creative drama teacher, Jean Stuart.

Spread your creepy crawly leaves
Over the fall—rock wall
Waves come splashing o'er the eaves
Push you and you fall.

Watch the sea creature drift by—an undulating eel, a drifting gossamer jellyfish, a gaudy lobster.
The waters of the sea are taking them somewhere.

And when you have taken shape—you will grow and multiply—you will move and move until you form gardens of seaweed. A flower-like anemone may float in and hide and withdraw her green tentacles.
Curve and dive, quiver and float—
Spotted fish will gape.

You will make more movement—sinuous, or short and jerky or small and enfolding.
You will resist the pull of the waves. Work hard to protect yoûrself—the movement of the tides is increasing—
the stirring restlessness of the sea.
water movements are going to uproot you
you will feel the strength of the approaching waves—they engulf you and uproot you and you will be hurled on to the sand.
And there the sun will burn you—
     to shrivel and shrivel and die.

Prisoners of the Deep—*Carolyn*

    Almost like a giant, white hand
    foaming fingers clutch the sand.
    Cockles, winkles, start to slide,
    Caught in the first of the ebbing tide.

    Carried to the doleful deep,
    Swept out to the restless sea.
    Currents whirl and swirl and hurl
    One and all through the treacherous squall.

    Bashed against the mountainous rocks
    A clump of seaweed blocks
    Our path
    Entwined again we're caught
    New hope for escape is sought.

    And now 'tis calm—the storm has passed
    The wind has died—peace at last
    Our resting place—in the settling sand
    But still in the grip of the mighty hand.

Once again in the shifty shallows,
In the cliffs, dank caves gulp, swallow
Creeping
Crawling,
The giant white hand
Returns its captives back to land.

Francene—*Aged fourteen*

Seaweed, seaweed, seaweed green.
Hide in the water or you'll be seen;
Your pool is small, it is not deep
And against the edges you will creep.

The human being whom you dread
will find you and take you and you'll be dead
But that could not happen in your little pool
that could not happen to you.

But alas, it has!
They've taken you—from your pool
and thrown you onto the hot sand
and you have shrivelled up
and died an awful death.

Pam—*Year eight*

Little seaweed once a seed
Clings to the rock with endless greed;
The stringy seaweed now is rough
Rolling . . . Stringy stuff.

It sways like the sea
As if impatient to be free;
The rock is crushing its green smooth skin,
And now 'tis dying like a fish without its fin.

The seaweed lurches
Now it crouches out on the sea
. . . washed to eternity.

5 The Exploration of Pattern and Design in Movement Through the Colour Relationship of Chalk Drawings (A Creative Art Activity)[22]

Divide the class into equal groups.
Distribute sheets of large white drawing paper to each group.

The groups may choose two different coloured chalks. Later, if you want to continue developing the relationship between drawing and dance design, more colours can be used.

Paint can later be used expressing colour lines and shapes or just the way you feel—big splashes of colour, different kinds of lines, very thin watery paint, or very dry brush strokes.

We start by drawing a few simple shapes. Each girl in the group adds a line or shape and then passes on her chalks to the next girl.
Make your drawing spontaneous!
Choose the colours which suit your idea
If you have made a mistake turn it into another kind of idea.
Try to draw with one continuous line

Each girl in her group should be following the idea and development of the design.
Make your design abstract and make it simple.
Don't worry if your design looks irregular or lopsided.
Each group has the same amount of time to complete their drawing.

We start off by hanging the drawings so that everyone can view them and the class can participate in analysing and interpreting the ideas.

You probably won't like every drawing; there may be some parts of them that you like especially.

The drawings need not remind you of anything—you might like the use of colours—or the good design.

22 This idea was based on a similar task during my experience in a Creative Arts Seminar at New York University, U.S.A. 1960.

Look closely—look at the whole shape

Space

Design

Rhythm

Colour relationships

Intention of the group

Look for common or distinct features in each drawing.
Look at the different parts of the drawing.
What do you think of the designs?

Most of the groups agreed that there was a certain similar use of dynamics
—that the sensitive, changing, dynamic lines were the most expressive.

Another group drew reflected spatial awareness, simple bold outlines which
merely suggested the form.
Softness and calmness suggested by the use of delicate colours, curving lines—
Red and black thrusting lines, direction and movement, and if translated into
dance design the point of attention would be through the diagonal line—
decisive straight lines and geometrical directness.

One almost looks like a nature landscape—with colour and shape of rocks.

Some of the designs look like doodling with many quick small lines.

Leonie, *a year nine student, comments:*

"I think most of the drawings are original. Most groups had an idea and tried
to express it. I did not think much of the designs where only one kind of line
was used. Where different lines were used such as squiggles, curves and straight
lines, the effect was more varied."

Susan:

"Out of the 8 group drawings only 2 looked to me to be purely abstract.
They looked to me like a graph of all the curving movements we had done
that day. The others did have a basic shape but they did not develop the
shape enough to make an interesting or exciting pattern.
    "At first, the peculiar squiggles on the sheets of paper looked like just a waste
of time, paper and chalk. The green curves intersected by red and dots were
confusing lines.
    "However, after thoughtfully looking at the patterns I seemed to see
fantastic designs for weird insects."

Helen:

"A thick sweeping line from one corner of the drawing paper to the other seemed to be a dancer's body curving in a wide strong movement. The lines scrunched in tiny, confined spaces were like people hiding from some danger."

"The lines that we drew in our group seemed like people curving and stretching; legs, arms, the back were expressed by our colours which blended and yet contrasted so that there was a pattern of movement."

* * *

Can you suggest ways of moving that will emphasise the colour, shapes and arrangement of your ideas? This dance-drawing study should express the structure of the chalk design and direct fluid movement.

Now build your relationship in dance from the designs on paper, transferring it to your own bodies on the floor and in the air. Will your design use the space or will it be close in a mass?

Will you use curved or straight lines?

Will your design be an abstract or does it have an idea?

The design could be a series of isolated movements or could the movements be linked?

You can merge static positions with moving passages of movement in your design.

Try to convey the idea and feeling for movement that you had in your chalk design through your body.

Do not be casual—show no emotion—only effective design.

Will it be a design for 5 or 6 bodies? Consider how the group can be divided— 3 + 2, 1 + 4, 2 + 2 + 1, or 5 single bodies.

Try out all possible combinations.

The diagonal line is the strongest line you can make in space.

Try to find the line and dynamics appropriate to the design.

Work to counts—a phrase of 32 counts, showing rhythmic development, any symmetry or asymmetry in the design. In symmetry, everything is equal—one part of the body is equal to the other. This gives a reposeful harmonious feeling—tranquillity and contentment.

So find smooth, rounded movement; use curves, serene sweeping curves of the body backwards, sideways and circular.

Circle the arms lyrically from inside to outside; out to in; across the body; arms can move separately or together.

Youthful and rich successional movement (successional—one movement succeeded by the next and the next without interruption) gives a feeling of continuous flow. The body unfolds as in a forward, backward or sideways wave. Arms, body and legs can all be connected with the ripple through the back wave with one leg in a high forward developpé.

If you have isolated patterns in your chalk drawing try to reflect the isolation in movement.

A head turning, a leg circling, arms rotating, one shoulder only moving perhaps up and down, in and out—lay stress on each of the parts of the body but keep in mind the total effect.

Focus on one part of the body and explore the possibilities of movement.

Move separately or together, and utilise connecting movements or transitions.

Texture and vitality can be accentuated in movement by percussive use of the body—these movements do not dissipate themselves but all the drama, vigour, vitality is contained in the sudden contracting and release—this percussive movement is a segment of a curve and contains power and force of movement.

Even if you have straight lines, vertical, horizontal or diagonal and curves, you can still have an ordered balance in bodily design.

In this movement phrase whether softly undulating, rhythmical or with dynamic accents, try to give it a sense of completeness—a beginning, a middle and an end.

As each dance study was shown we found different things to praise and to criticise.

Contents were skilfully organised and the phrasing thoughtful, but some cliché and repetitive movements crept into the designs.

There were well-designed patterns of straight, angular and curved bodies in movement and an attempt at spaciousness in the designs. Some designs were elegant and there was some gradation of bodies as they related to each other.

There was an intensity of effort to translate the movement of line and colour, with directional and spatial patterns evident in the drawings—into a design for bodies and movement.

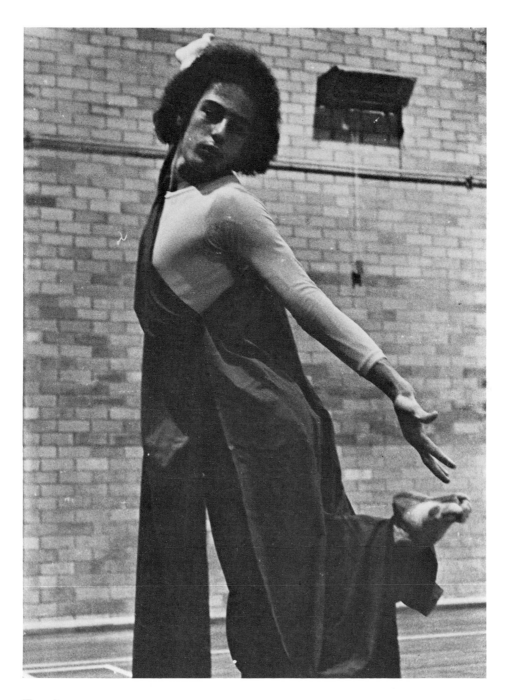

Tension

6   The People's Walk

A visual progression—the recreation and stylising of an ordinary human activity—the walk.

The entire class of thirty-five, boys and girls take part—all walking—a mass in action.

The form will evolve from the content.
The figures begin to move across the floor—across the space—a loose mass—at first all move in the same direction—people on the move—children, youth, old age in joy, weariness, heaviness, happiness and strength.

As the walk progresses;[23] it reveals some surprising rhythms. Each individual describes his own individual rhythm of walking within a larger rhythm of movement—quicker and quicker, some are slow, almost slow motion in their steps, some pass and re-pass, the walk of some is bouncy, light and springy, some drag and shuffle their feet.
The walk from birth to death—
Acceleration or almost to a standstill—it never stops. Some figures thread their way through the mass, across the space and back. Each finds her own direction, many keep walking in the one direction. There are some encounters then a change of direction to avoid collisions. The ripple of the walk; erect figures using their feet, arches, ball of the foot and toes, ankles and insteps, arms swinging, bodies well stretched up, chests lifted, legs moving freely; bodies pulled forward by gravity; the inward and downward curve; heaviness in the step, bent legs, arms released, heads hanging—no resistance. Some kneel to the floor and crawl. The pattern is created by those who walk from birth to death.

The faces reflect their feelings—some show detachment, expressionless, absorbed in their own world of introspection. There is an air of aloofness from some, on other faces I see expressions of concern and protectiveness All have a collective state of mind—in their lives they will love and hate, hope and fear and aspire. This binds them together and there is an aura of fellowship. The only sound is the feet.

My words and phrases follow the action of the moving mass. It is their accompaniment.

23 This theme was given at Fort Street High School, to boys and girls; years Seven and Eight.

Gestures evolve; figures stop, support each other; the pair walk together—
the lines suggest grief or age.

—an endless procession—

The everlasting walk,

exhausting sorrow, draining all strength,

The burden on one's back, legs;

The living death that weighs down the walk.

The walk of people, of life.

Toward the end of the piece some figures are still moving, some very slowly,
and others still quickly about and some are still just standing silently and some
are lying—and the moving figures weave in and out—all part of the movement
of people.

This theme was done by a year seven class of 12 and 13 year olds—boys and
girls. I walked onto the floor in the middle of the thirty-five students, and as
we walked, I began to talk and describe the idea. I could feel the reacton being
quite clearly expressed in the shape.

7 HAIKU

"The blossoms beckon pink, blood red,

While I sit dumb

In this high white room."

The Poetic Material of Japanese Haiku: (an inspiring source for interpretation into movement.)

A small group of us studied the characteristics of classical haiku; the rhythm and stress of the syllables; the references to nature and the seasons; the mention of an event and the way the event is expressed with great simplicity and immediacy—some of the group attempted to compose their own haiku.

Lynden, a gifted year eleven student, illustrated the emotion and the whole picture more clearly than others. The members of the dance group also felt that they could convey in movement, to some extent, the meaning of Lynden's haiku.

The task was to make sure that these fleeting impressions were captured by the phrases of dance movement—certainly not all poetry can be translated into movement and, in haiku, the dancer's action should break through the confinement of the word—and be able to evoke the mood or emotional atmosphere by an appropriate choice of movements.

Lynden assisted the group in their choice of movements and outlined her depth of meaning behind each haiku—

> Sky-bird pierce the dawn
> Releasing my cold, cold soul
> To the kiss of Sun.

"A picture I always carry in my mind of the coming of Spring, the coming of warmth, the coming of love."

> Tom-Cat, my suave friend
> Scamper through the leaf-strewn ways
> Morning—you'll sleep on.

"The next door pedigree lapping up his domestic comforts yet as sly as any alley-cat in the pursuit of pleasures."

> Boys and fire-flies
> Take the bullfrog from his rest
> Lovely squelching mud.

"I always see my brother and his associates; playing rough boyish games, boasting of adventures catching tadpoles."

> Swaying bamboo shoots
> Bow their heads to harsh breezes—
> Delicate dancers.

"The vitality and lyricism of nature embodied for me in the skill and graces of the dancer."

> Frostmen paint the wood with
> shiny stinging fingers
> Alas butterfly.

"The whiteness and cruelty of winter as it freezes over the landscape. The poor delicate colourful creatures like the butterfly are crushed by the piercing cold and the ruthlessness of Man."

Drawn up from my heart
Songs of past children's summers—
Old woman's moaning.

"I was influenced by Arnold Bennett who gives a most depressing picture of old age."

We had to shape the content.

The ones who felt compelled to work out the haiku for themselves in terms of dance began to work with the stanza that they understood.

I spoke to them about trying to work outside themselves, to find a new self through the verse—that one must feel the air movements of the sky-bird; understand the humour of the cats; one must be touched by the sadness of old age and glimpse its memories; one must be able to let us hear the oozing of mud—the blows of men in the forest and the deathliness of icy wastes; one must be able to reveal the tenuous grace of the dancer.

Each one must struggle to recognize the meaning and to respond enough so that the meaning and quality of the different haiku will be drawn out in the dance.

The haiku verses were spoken by one of the dancers who was familiar with the expressive qualities of the haiku and the rhythm and flow of movement. In her lyrical voice she accompanied the dancers so that the words and movement became an integral part of each other.

Different dance-students chose different haiku verses and two figures worked together in "Frost Men". Ideas began to evolve as to the choice of movement needed to express the ideas and themes.

A simple form should evolve, evocative of the meaning of each haiku.

Jumps with flexed feet and rhythmic dartings of arms and quick changes of direction suggested the mischievous pranks in "Boys and Fireflies". Then crude awkwardness as the body rolled and crawled along the ground to give the feeling of being enveloped in the heaviness of mud.

A long wished-for freedom by the one as "sky-bird"—soaring through the space, identifying with the free wheeling movements of birds. She felt that she would not suffer any longer from spiritual poverty if she could achieve freedom and see a means of doing so in the swift action of flying.

Pathos and loneliness in the dejected inward curving of the old women— The bent figure swathed in black material imaginatively moved through misery to the hopelessness of old age; there the inward pull of the body shapes changed and the lines of movement became strong purposeful and vital. Memory awakened as the figure of childhood moved with leaps, balances, and fast out-stretched extensions. A controlled slowing down and the dynamism is replaced by movement with static qualities—and the inevitability of age is heightened by a pendulum-like rocking of the crouching body.

Archings and twistings of the body; curvings around the back sinuously depict the movements of the cat. Explosive jumps with feet drawn high under the body, legs bent, infused into the movement, sudden thrusts of energy.

Sly off-beat humour was reflected in the facial expression and quaint irregular pawings and shuffling of the feet and hands.

58

The sustained quality of the long graceful lines of the arabesque—delicate curvings of the head, neck and arms—the undulating rhythm of the back wave, light runs arrested once more into the supple unfolding rhythm of the line of the back. Balances with the repose of symmetry—no tautness or harsh lines here but a harmonious composition created by fluid movements.

The cruelty of nature reflected in the "Frost Figure"[24]—wide stance, archaic[25] lines of movement, vigorous and strong two-dimensional lines—the whole body is taut, and aware of each movement. Even the fingers are spread wide as the arms are outstretched forward and upward. Strong thrusts of the leg in front or to the side with the foot flexed—all the lines are straight with tensions and the figure expresses force—there is always a deliberate design relationship between the arms and legs.

The butterfly with curved, light movements has a delicate quality—her flutterings become more fragmented and finally the movement of her wings is broken by a single sharp cutting movement by the "Frost Figure".

*   *   *

Criticism of dance studies of Haiku

The teacher needs to approve and encourage the original creative effort. Then instruction, meaningful correction, should follow to assist the students towards further creative adventures.

"More energy in the jumps—the cat must be more springy. Curve your hands and arms—use them like paws—more sly humour—show it through the movement. Don't just grin."

Mud, mud, mud, the feeling of earth slimy, roll in it. Don't be so ladylike—nothing dainty.

Can you, as the bird-figure, give us the sense of soaring—higher. Your feet look like feet—more twist in the feet—like a bird's claw.

Air Design . . . you have to achieve an awkward grace . . . no, it is not natural. . . .

Try hopping, on one foot only . . . not just on one spot . . . now dart . . . dart . . . now use your head but with tension and in short sharp jerky movements . . . your arms look as if they are practising semaphore. . . . Now balance and find a rhythm with your arms—balance asymmetrically . . . taut . . . that's it . . .

24 From Lynden's Haiku, "Frost Men".

25 *Modern Dance Forms*—by Louis Horst—The Archaic, p. 69/74. (Impulse Publications, San Francisco.)

59

Let me see the CAT again . . . arch your back. . . . Slink—now creep on the floor . . . now in walking . . . use your feet . . . where is the spring . . . sudden, unpredictable . . . that is good!

If you intend to dance show me the line of your legs . . . the back . . . use the half-toe . . . more lightness . . . more lightness . . . You are too static . . . use the space. . . . Don't look as if you are saying "cheese". . .

A lovely lyrical ending. . . . Deepen your bend, small movements of the hands from the wrists and controlled balance . . .

FROST FIGURE feel your stance on the floor . . . plant your feet on the floor and feel the tension through to your fingertips . . .

Control the body . . . hollow it . . . feel pulled in. . . . If you are using black material on the Figure of Old Age it must become part of the figure not simply adornment . . . narrow gestures. . . . Now in memory of Youth—unfold, expand . . . large . . . wide . . . joyful movement . . . I must be moved when you sink once more into the shrunken position of the hopeless . . .

DO NOT simply translate the poetry word for word. . . . Be strict with yourself. . . . Do not make any extraneous gestures. . . . Think of the spoken accompaniment as a musical accompaniment . . . try to assemble your feelings about your haiku . . . as your phrases of movements are connected, there the form will appear.

There will be a variety of artistic forms . . . unless the studies are designed mechanically and I hope that they are NOT . . . then I should experience the total expression of the Haiku studies that are being communicated to me through movement.

8 Sound

Charles Ives, a twentieth-century American composer, has this to say:
"that he himself has often stretched the limits of musical expression to the utmost; and it is the listener who needs to be bold and adventurous in attempting to follow him." For as Ives writes: "Beauty in music is too often confused with something that lets the ears lie back in an easy chair. Many sounds that we are used to, do not bother us, and for that reason, we are inclined to call them beautiful." Ives remarks that familiar sounds, like drugs, can be habit-forming.[26]

26 *America's Music*—Gilbert Chase (McGraw-Hill), Chapter 31, p. 657.

You live in a wide range of realistic sound suggested by conditions in the modern world. Many sounds that bothered your parents no longer have any effect on you.

The clanging sharpness of the industrial scene, the concatenation of sound produced by mechanisation, the noise range thrust at us in radio and television sound effects—from thunderclaps and explosions to shrieks and groans.

We live in a vortex of an immense variety of sound material. It would take a mingling of sounds so dissonant or out of harmonic relation to disconcert and distract our attention today; so accustomed are we becoming to the strange world of sounds.

Lie down on the floor—

One layer of sound added to another.

Clock sounds, ringing, ticking.

Pots and pans clanging.

Human sounds, the baby, the time; the pop record.

Street noises.

The grind of transportation.

Dynamic noise of the city—Someone is cutting steel—The humans are the movement and the sound is the accompaniment.

Sound. Silence.

And now stretch your EARS.

You are lying in the middle of Sound.

Listen to the sounds in the space around you.

Shrieking, trumpeting, changing, whining and grinding.

The machine-gun insistence of the drill.

Is there such a thing as silence?

Does sound communicate?

Noise and Sound.

The pattern of Sound is always changing as life is changing.

Can we make a sound composition?

Can you utter a sound or are you swallowed up and silenced by the sounds around you?

Be free and explore Sound.

Use the voice, lips, tongue, cheeks. Now try harsh hard sounds, staccato sounds, whistling sounds, buzzing sounds, grunting sounds and low-pitched sounds, rubbing sounds, long-sustained sounds and short sounds.

Now search out some expressive sounds with the fingers, hands, feet and body.

Can you involve yourself in your sounds enough to work out convincing movements so that there is an artistic synthesis of sounds and movement?

Now form groups of three to six and design a group sound-movement pattern.

Your sound phrase should have a time span, some organisation of dynamics of movement and position in space. You may begin and finish at any given time taking care that your sound and movement are part of a balanced whole. Each group then shares a collective variation of sound. As each group goes to work on the study there could be a great deal of noise; however, gradually the conglomeration of sound subsides and the groups organise their sound phrase in the way in which they want to.

I have found that when a class is intent upon a creative activity, one can expand this growing sense of creativity by a sympathetic recognition of their work. Give to the child and to the group a feeling that they have developed something imaginative and original.

Be ready to assist with suggestions if you are asked. The study may need more manipulation of material to carry the idea through or someone may be technically unskilled and may need to find the right kind of movement that is suitable for them.

The child reveals something of herself and her needs in her work. If you *impose* your ideas they will ignore your suggestions, feeling them to be a hindrance to their inventiveness.

The reaction of the class to the first experiment with sound could be a painful one. No one need budge and there could be a great reluctance to utter one sound.

Sounds will emerge timidly at first. Listen for the smallest sound.

Give clues—

Loudness—softness, short, sharp, jerky;

Suck in the breath.

Use your tongue, teeth, lips and breath.

Laugh, grunt, shout.

Make commonplace sounds.

Make them expressive—vital sound NOT half-hearted sounds.

Each individual will want to release their own sound and they will find it amusing.

Let them experiment with sound recklessly.

Then you can call a halt.

Refine your sound. Choose what you want to say and design movement to fit.

Small delicate hand gestures for diminishing hushed tones.

Short sharp dynamics to express percussive, staccato bursts of sound.

Closing to opening or from narrow to wide movements of the arms or a recovery from the floor to standing might suggest a swelling crescendo of sound.

Parts of the body moving separately for diverse rhythmic sound and pitch variation.

And when the groups merge there should not be a casual accompaniment but a rich combination of fragments of sound each weighted according to pitch, tone, variety and duration.

*　　*　　*

FOUND-SOUND

"Why with the time do I not glance aside to new-found methods and to compounds strange?"

William Shakespeare
Sonnet LXXVI

The class can bring in "found-sound"[27] varying from natural objects to man-made.

Any sound is legitimate.

We have the ability to distinguish through the human ear the millions of sounds around us. Each sound has a distinctive pitch, loudness and quality.

Divide the class into groups with each individual playing their own sound and then fuse the individual sounds into a simple combination. The sources of sound are wide and various and many have a basic musical character but whatever sounds are chosen the students' efforts will be unique only if they experiment and learn to use the Techniques of Tape Recording. Information about these Tape Recording Techniques can be supplied by a record or tape recording company.

Here are some of the techniques using one or two tape recorders.
1. Variation in Tape Speed and Pitch (some sounds appear higher or lower to our ears than others).
2. Reversing play-backs.
3. Tape—Looping.
4. Reverberations and echo effects.
5. The use of filters for music and speech and the effect of overtones on sound filters.

A knowledge of how the sound is changed and reversed with pauses and percussive effects can be then achieved on the tape recorders with a simple knowledge and familiarity with the acoustic phenomena. You can lighten, darken your composition, express tones, speeds and qualities. There will be discussion about sequence development and the need to fit sounds together; contrast a beginning and end, silence, harmony, balance and the dynamic colours of the sound sequence.

27 Found-Sound, an Experimental Topic in Dance and the Related Arts, New York University, U.S.A., 1960.

Tape record each group's composition.
Ask questions:
Too much repetition?

Was there an over-all shape?

Were you limited by your imagination?

Was the sequence improvised or was it arranged in a simple form and did it explore sound?

Could you identify the captured sounds?

Some of the students agreed that they were limited by selection of raw material and by the lack of imaginative organisation of sound—others achieved a startling synchronisation of sounds.
We identified—

Coughs, laughter

a clock striking

road drills

vocal sounds, hush, sh sh, ohs, psstt, purrs, ahs

kitchen utensils, spoons, egg-beater

water poured into a glass.

"Thunder", illustrated by sheets of brass being undulated slowly and sinuously, then hard and fast. Whistles.
There were continuous or rolling sounds, dry and percussive sounds.

Bells

Tuning fork

Metronome beat

Talking—laughter recorded at different speeds

Vibrations produced by the plucking of a taut violin string

French songs

Paper rustling

The ease and success with which beginners handle this material interpreting sounds and found-sound, depends on the degree of technical skill, practice in improvisation and previous creative experience. The time you will spend developing this project will be in relation to your "goals".

As this is an experiment in another area of dance with different subject matter then movements should be of the kind best suited to express the qualities of sound.

It may be an experiment whereby the compositions are organised into a simple intelligible form—or following the exploratory sounds with more inter-action by the group. The rhythmic pulse of the phrase can be expressed by the use of rhythm either by movements arising from the Breath Rhythm[28] with its rise and fall of movement through the rise and fall of the breath—sharp intakes of breath and the even movement can be broken, sharp and strong. If there is a rhythmic shape in the sound phrase, the group should delight in the sensory feeling of rhythmic movement through the use of Metric Rhythm.[29]

Changes of rhythm and combinations will make the student alert—even a monotonous beat can be exciting; a metronome; be aware of the rhythmic complexities, combinations and patterns in life around us. In the walk, run and jump—in the world of nature and in the human experience. Try a sound rhythm like the ritualistic changing of the guard; the movement of a soldier; actions in sport; the rhythm of a blind man walking—listen to the different rhythms of age and occupations!

Any dimension of sound can be projected into space so that there is an awareness of line, curved or linear, focus, direction (sideways, diagonal, circular). The body can explore the space around it; the movement of the feet can create a floor pattern and the body can extend itself vertically, horizontally, in a spiral, move in a circle, changing the direction and level. A floor rhythm as in shifting weight forward and backward or side to side.

If you stimulate the interest of your class to further exploration and guide them in the use of some of the compositional devices I have talked about, a form with feeling and character can become apparent in the presentation of their ideas.

To obtain the value of a sound listen to what it is, just as it is.

Listen to the Sounds in Space around you.

One morning Lucinda wove her pattern of Sound for us and gave me her poem.

She infused into her movement the subtle variations of softness, loudness, the piercing harshness of the sweep and purity of sound. Like a plant she moved across the floor, gentle and indolent. Her accompanying sounds were well modulated but quiet—rippling legato movements. Fragment by fragment the dance movement unfolded and passed away—elusive.

Sounds and shapes merged—were extricated more feverish and strident—altered, diminished, amplified into new resonances. She twisted and melted like a candle. As we sat, we were conscious of the expanded life of the imagination.

Her vocal and tactile sounds led her to stamp, to prance, to explosions of sound and movement—the animated joyous leap—or calm and frail droning and gliding;

Motionless, silent, frozen, her shape hung like some ancient ship stranded upon the shore.

*   *   *

28 Doris Humphrey.

29 Gertrud Bodenwieser.

66

Poem by Lucinda, *aged 15 years*

sound and movement
sound and movement
sliding, gliding, finding myself.
turning with force
swerving and curving
a stretched hand a supple back
the long smooth neck—the perfect line
of sound and movement.
sparkling, bubbling, spelling, hissing
slow movement. Slow movement
slow with slime and grease and grime.
slippery wet, dry as a bone
slide together, stop the soldier follows,
they have sound and movement—
but not like ours. theirs is set—set
Rhythm, set beat, set step—they
cannot have slow movement.
their movement is quick, lively, thoughtless
each step follows another. a set pattern
of stamping feet.
our steps are light
sometimes not graceful, but what is grace?
we dance what we feel, how we feel.

Time . . . .
The grains of time fall slowly,
ever so slowly when we wish
the steady stream of sand mounts
and forms a mountain of time.
each tiny grain of sand is a milestone.
and when the last grain drops
so the last milestone turns a millstone
around our memories
to be cast into the deep, blue sea
I feel a cool violet
and yet I dislike my clumsiness so full of
emotion am I.
that I am tearing in half with
hate and pity and jealousy
and love
That yet because I feel this separation
of body and soul; neck and body
that I am two
two separate halves already.

A chilling blast is felt.
It sends blue shivers down my soul
The blast grows stronger and stronger
heavier, colder and fiercer,
the blue stings like
freezing, fangs of hate.

Cold hate.

the dropping silence is heard
yet the chilling blasts go on wilder and fiercer
taking more and more
leaving remains static
the corners creep out like cold, smooth
        fingers,
reaching, grasping, taking, having
while the centre is a swirling mass of
confusion,
Advancing, with drawing,
flying, rushing to . . . of nothing
running, falling, tumbling
        always going.
always going to infinity.
before profound, now tranquil,
from solemn and subdued
to passive and serene.
the enchanting nothingness of this world
is only felt after a storm
storm of torrents, of rain and thunder
storm of thought, lurking in the crevice of one's mind
gathered and left standing
until capacity of the mind
bursts at the seams
and thoughts rush like torrents of water
through eyes and mind and consciousness
surging, swirling, rapids of chaos
till reaching neutral waters
restful, afflicted, retired
is resigned to flow on, negatively
to callow youth; youth of greenness
raw and immature youth,
fresh and contemplative youth.

*   *   *

Aerodybulide

Dance group members, Janet and Angela, experimented further with a more complex dance study in sound.

The thematic material was a concrete chemistry experiment stylised as a dance and with a found-sound accompaniment. Their own special level of ability after four years training in the modern dance gave them the assurance to amplify their ideas with tape recording accompaniment. They designed the work for four dancers—Janet, Angela, Lisa and Frances,[30] the composers.

"The theme is based on a reaction between acid on a carbonate."

"To begin we had to decide whether our idea was an effective theme for a dance. It should not be a literal transalation of the scientific aim but we wanted to express the essence of the chemical changes—.

"The changes are dynamic and we had to trap the characteristic sounds."

"The component parts of the music are fireworks, amplified vocal sound, traffic sounds, water and silence. Working with two tape recorders, and a microphone we amplified sound, recorded it at different speeds, distorted sound and edited the tape; this took hours of work."

"The basis of the dance was extracted from the idea of the metamorphosis from limestone and acid to water, carbon dioxide and a salt (symbolised as mechanism).

"The duration of the dance work was six minutes—we invented the word 'Aerodybulide' as an expressive title for our dance work."

The material was still rough and unpolished when I was asked to see whether a form or structure was taking place. Was there a development?

Unity

Dynamics

Content

An over-all shape?

or awareness and proper use of space-relationships?

The individual or a group should be placed in the space in relation to other bodies in the spatial area.

Working on these premises the group structured the dancework. They did NOT accept any movements or designs that were superimposed. ALL had to grow organically from the idea and the kind of movement that they were capable of making.

An effective and original piece of work became more and more apparent but to me what lifted it above the level of a mediocre piece of work was the conviction with which they performed it. The Figure of Salt (Janet) gave the work a bitter intensity.

30 Year Ten, average age 15 years.

These dance students sought, within the limits of their knowledge and technical range, a satisfying expressive work which had the power to communicate.

The climax with its moment of impact is at the beginning as the solid group is attacked by the Figure of Acid; who with wild broken asymmetrical movement thrusts into the group. The mass disintegrates and forms new interlocking shapes. As the unified structure of the group is dissolving the mood changes and becomes scintillating and effervescent—movements become rhythmic, gay, light. The fluid movement by the Figure of Water has a floating, lyrical quality that contrasts with the relentless staccato movement of the two figures as Salt. A clenched fist opening and closing gives us the indication that changes are arrested only momentarily—new breakdowns will occur and new relationships emerge.

*   *   *

Ionisation

"I do not write experimental music. My experimenting is done before I make the music. Afterwards, it is the listener who must experiment."[31]

Find a place on the floor:
Sit or lie in a position where you can
        LISTEN,   BE AWARE,   FEEL,   LISTEN

I introduced Ionisation by Varese, an uncompromising composer of the twentieth century. Throughout the piece there were foot tappings and movements of the hands by some of the students as they reacted to the rhythmical structure. The score is written for percussion and among the instruments used are maraccas, bells, gongs, triangles, drums and high and low sirens. Its strong underlying expressive element is a result of Varese's dynamic organisation of the sound.

I had some misgivings. Should one put this work of such sonorous texture before the class? Can they comprehend or can they NOT comprehend—"His strange world of sounds in which primitive forces blend with the dynamic energy of the modern industrial city."[32]

Yet in order to bring out fresh and exciting qualities in the creative achievements by the class there has to be continual involvement on an improvisatory scale.

To put this sound experience into movement, you need time to absorb and assemble the sound vocabulary—to make your choice as to how you will create your dance response.

Some of the students from years nine, ten and eleven, generate ideas—others are uncertain about their reaction and one may need to play the Ionisation again—separate passages and then the entire work—before they will discover

31 A comment on his musical composition by Edgar Varese; American Composer.

32 *America's Music* by Gilbert Chase. McGraw-Hill Publishing Co.

some order and pattern in the sound arrangement and be stimulated to find a meaning for themselves.

"A Science-Fiction horror."

The sounds seem to be fighting against each other.

Panic—confusion.

A princess imprisoned in a tower.

Japanese Theatre.

Inside a watch.

Frightenining—no feeling.

Demolition.

Kitchen utensils coming to life.

Claustrophobic—a trapped feeling—you keep trying to find a way out.

Ancient Arabian music.

The Release of Energy.

Brutal Music.

A kind of madness.

The bells suggest peace—as if you were lying in an open space—there is a feeling of tranquillity.

City life.

Just noises?

Hurling oneself into space.

Anything can happen!

White Ice . . .

Reassured by your understanding and insight into the creative situation, the dance student will want to talk about her ideas. Also that you communicate to each individual the freedom to express her thoughts and feelings about a musical composition, painting or poetry or a phase of life—this will make her confident in her verbal statements. Then the rest of the class can participate;

listening to or discussing the peculiar differences in the ideas. At this point we will be ready to ask—will the concept make good dance material and can the creative manifestation of that conception communicate to us?

Here in this world of Improvisation the students experiment—feet flexed, bodies twisted into strange distorted shapes, arms moving so that they say something; the leg turned in or turned out as the body contracts and releases. To think in terms of pure movement, using the body in fantastic knotted shapes or in long cool planal lines as the body moves unconsciously from one plane to the next. One must be careful to channel the improvisations in a way that is consistent with the disciplines of the modern dance. This art form is concerned with finding new ways of registering dance—we must continually think in terms of describing the pulse of our time—tension, speed, restlessness.

In the manipulation of material in the modern dance there is little decoration; a sparseness and a clarity; there is dissonance and asymmetry, no sentiment, not always a happy or peaceful ending; an alertness, a sense of urgency and enquiry—always moving—moving for the first time; almost the sense of the inarticulate in our movements; as Martha Graham calls it—"The divine awkwardness"; like the movements of a young child simple and direct and not concerned with superficialities. To intensify their accomplishments in this way there must be further opportunity for the class to work on their improvisational studies—to explore more deeply the ways in which they can experiment with Ionisation. Without a conscious shaping of the students' intentions into organised movement experimentation, formlessness can occur, as one listens to this barrage of sound!

In the space dance students work on their studies—individually or in small groups.

Those watching are able to appraise, analyse and criticise the creative efforts. They are in the process of knowing what to look for in a dance work and how to achieve it through—The change of level or focus or direction; more invention with the arm; meaningless movement should be discarded; invert the phrase; use the spatial area—expand your floor pattern or minimise your working area.

Too often the dance student finds herself limited by her technique or hampered because of POOR imagination and threadbare content—OR again she could be overburdened by her idea and not have sufficient skill to shape the content: OR the idea may simply be untranslatable into dance.

How successful you become in nurturing the creative spirit will depend on you—The smallest creative achievement by any member of the class must never be ignored. Each individual should be concentrating on finding ways to express and to invent.

If the ideas are subjective try to relate them to life so that the dance student is aware of the universal breadth of the idea. To develop these creative studies aesthetically, more assimilation by the class would be required with reference to an increased sensitivity about the scope of the music, and a further awareness of the aesthetic forms of the dance. These forms will successfully allow the private vision that each girl has about Ionisation to be translated into movement in a conceivable and convincing way: not a naked revelation of the individual's innermost needs and desires, but a coherent expression of the emotion in some recognisable form.

We find some of the theories of the art form of the modern dance controlling the work.

The arthitectonic element in Varese's Ionisation can be described in movement as a striving for tension with emphasis on the lines of stress. The physical pull of one part of the body moving against another part. There is no relaxation or dying between movements. It is this deliberate pull of the body that can express a purpose—to show tensions created by conflict within an individual.

Feel the body pulling one part against the other. Slowly through the whole body, motion gives way to emotion "One can have a sense of wonder and awe —awe is almost the beginning of fear".[33]

Stand on right foot—lift left leg in front—the left foot is flexed.

Left arm presses downwards—left hand flexed. Right hand on back of neck, slowly and deliberately press on the back of the neck and head bends. Step back on left leg—right leg slowly lifted back and right foot is flexed.

Head lifts but there is tension in the neck as it resists the right hand. Step on right leg and brush left leg sharply across the front of the body (stretched left leg) and then lift it slowly and deliberately to left diagonal back and tilt the body right diagonal forward—walk the hands down the right leg and then reach back with the left leg as it is placed on the floor to take the weight on the left knee, draw the right leg in with right hip out until the right foot is close to the left knee. Contract the body, twisting it towards the right knee, and kneel sit on the left foot.

This is unimaginable unless there is a slow physical pull—one leg pulling against the other—the body striving to resist the space as it tilts, the only quick sharp movement is the left leg brushing across the body.

Just as Varese is absorbed with his sonorities so the dance student should be aware of arranging her own planal concepts—the "Planal Consciousness"[34] eliminates natural movement and a strange and studied appearance in movement occurs—They are evenly spaced, exact and measured and there is an alertness and a sense of always moving as the body moves consciously from one plane to another.

If the leg is bent—bend the arm. If the leg lifts to the side and is straight, lift the same arm to the side. There is also a consciousness of space—a machine-like precision, as the movements are slowly and deliberately executed.

Through a study of the archaic form, one can become more sensitised to the planal lines of movement.

"This archaic form in dance is the formal arrangement of the body in two-dimensional lines, where every movement is given its full value—movement is arrested and goes with a strange tautness into the next movement. No sensuousness, no frills or curves but a deliberate feeling of tension and strength as one movement design connects to the next."[35]

33 Louis Horst—New York.

34 Louis Horst.

35 Louis Horst.

Strange design
Photograph: Douglas Thompson

"The music of Varese has the beauty and precision of an intricate machine and creates its emotion objectivly, not as a subjective projection of the composer's ego or a public display of his private feelings."[36]

The expression of certain states of feeling by the students could be embarrassing if they have not already been aware aware of how to indicate their emotion through the correct gesture or through a kinetic awareness of the body and its parts.

There is a danger of students becoming involved in themes that are too grandiose to handle—one girl could not dance war but she could arouse our sympathy by showing us a fear of war or some state that the results of war have induced in her.

If the idea then springs from the subjective—as a state of mind resulting from her innermost thoughts and feelings—this state can be objectified—her state of conflict or frustration or some other agonising feeling about fears and weaknesses can be expressed by well-chosen movements—but there must be no indulgence—no personalising.

One of my year eleven dance students, Jan, wrote after listening to Varese's composition "Ionisation"—

. . . "a person wandering, seeking more involvement with life—searching—He is discontented and wants freedom—a Modern Day Utopia. While he is searching he is happy enough but he is alone.

"The layers of soûnd in Ionisation are like the pressures of Society—all the Limitations."

We watched a manipulation of the planal concepts in movement in the expressive structure of some of the students' themes set to the musical score by Varese—they created a theme which expressed demolition—movements were deliberately arrested—planal body designs twisted and distorted as one part of the body pulled against the other—there were uneven, rhythmical jabbing movements, with focus on elbows, knees, hips, fingers, feet.

No collapsing movements, but a skyline of jagged, uneven, broken, designs—the arrangement of the shapes gave us a feeling of unrest.

One does not always want to be confronted by the continual struggles against suffering or to be immersed in the aversions, hostilities, or aggressive instinct of the individual—we sometimes need glimpse of harmless light topics, humorous, satire, zany, madcap.

Such as Advertising Slogans—

"Post No Bills"

"Caution"

"No Parking"

"Trespassers will be Prosecuted"

36 *America's Music* by Gilbert Chase, McGraw-Hill Book Publishing Co. Inc.

r Dance, Play, and Magic
ng Brown

"Stop . . . Go"

"Stop, Look and Listen"

"Curves"

"Warning"

Look in the newspaper columns, For Sale, Personal. One has to explore all possibilities of the simple themes—dehumanise the movement: no emotion, machinelike but with a sense of humour.

Not too long—no monotony unless you want to heighten the meaning—and a careful manipulation so that it is not repetitious.

The supreme beauty of the squares in Paul Klee's paintings are a visible representation of arrested movement. Symbols transform the landscape and nature, humanise objects, enchant us with a world of magic and fantasy—and in the moving simplicity of his geometric forms we are permitted a glimpse of the mind and the inner life of the man.

9 Concerning the elements of composition

The form and content are the two main streams in the structure of a dancework. The devices for carrying out these two aspects are "Rhythm, Design Gesture and Dynamics", according to Doris Humphrey whose theories on Choreography have now been published.

According to Louis Horst "manipulation of thematic material" was the device for composing movement. He has analysed his theories on composition in his writings; discussing the ways for the student of finding freedom to compose through the organisation of material according to a set of principles. Other teachers of composition[37] stress different approaches and attitudes stemming from their own training and experience—floor patterns, and spatial forms, line, harmony, balance, quality, force, unity, emotion, focus, level, dimension, curved, straight and broken lines, organic growth progression and transition, style. There are varying opinions and preferences, too, for the use of Design, Dynamics, Rhythm and Gesture and the importance they should play in achieving unity in a dance form. Yet in spite of the divergent views as to where the emphasis should be placed—on what element—the dance educators unanimously agree that dance composition is an important development in the programme of dance.

Teaching methods may be different and the choice of the elements of composition adapted to the needs of the students whether for solo or group work.

Compositional tasks should be kept simple to begin with, suiting the student's capabilities, technical standard and their artistic maturity. I have found that the simple well-defined creative task involving one element of composition is within the reach of students' experience with two or three years' technical and creative dance background.

Each new element should be selected carefully and with variety depending on the skill of the class and what they need to work on most.

"All dance movement" according to Suzanne Langer, "is gesture",[38] while Doris Humphrey talks of gesture as "the result of a feeling".[39]

Help the class to become aware and observant of the reactions and gestures of others. You will find descriptive photos in the newspapers—movements of parting and greeting; the joyful attitude of those who have won a prize; the despairing gestures and corresponding folding inwards of the body by those

37 Choreographers and Dance Lecturers in University Dance Departments, U.S.A.

38 *Feeling and Form* by Suzanne Langer. Charles Scribner Publishers, New York.

39 Doris Humphrey.

79

who are involved in a tragic situation—a woman turned out of her home or all her possessions destroyed by fire.

A study of these components in more demanding projects increases the skill for creative expression. The student has to make her intention clear; sort out movements and manipulate them meaningfully (an inventive use of arms with a turn or a jump); a new insight into ordering, placing and changing movement phrases; reassembling movements and phrases, and establishing transitions that flow and connect; an understanding by the student of her intention in organising her ideas.

10 CONSTRUCTIONS

"Any thing or action which enhances life, propels it

and adds to it something in the direction of growth,

expansion and development, is constructive. . . ."

Naum Gabo by Ruth Olsen and
Abraham Chanin

From GABO and PEVSNER
The Museum of Modern Art
New York City

"*I feel an artist* should go about his work simply with great respect for his materials. . . . Simplicity of equipment and an adventurous spirit in attacking the familiar or unknown. . . . In my own work when I began using wire as a medium I was working in a medium I had known since a child; for I used to gather up the ends of copper wire discarded when a cable had been spliced and with these and some beads would make jewellery for my sisters' dolls. . . ."[40]

Let us have a fresh viewpoint and explore our curiosity to the limit with certain types of materials—when we dance we are concerned with what our bodies will do for us. If we dance with a prop such as a fan, a basket, a crown, spear or cloak it is part of the character that we are dancing—a part of the role that we are creating or interpreting. It may also become a symbol for a deeper meaning, a means of expressing our ideas about the world we live in.

We have found that there are hundreds of things to dance about—and we have explored some of the creative ideas that have been submitted to me by the dance students during the years that I have been in this school—we have youth here, and because of this, energy, spontaneity, wit and stimulating ideas.

Students from years nine, ten and eleven were asked to construct forms that might express the ideas of our day choosing materials that could be applied in many ways—a chance to communicate their thoughts and feelings about the twentieth century.

They wanted to choose materials that would show the relationships of planes, shapes and patterns of the environment around us—and to comment on our twentieth century visual language through dance. The use of creative materials and often man-made objects linked with the planes, shapes and patterns made by the human body in movement, individually or in groups—in flat two-dimensional lines or three-dimensional designs.

Can we find the meaning in the new shapes which are becoming part of our environment—can we find meaning in the new structures—new lines in buildings, designs for furniture in the home, devices for making our lives more harmonious? Is it all just an entanglement of lifeless design that is valueless?

Can we find a new way of expressing ourselves; of perceiving the rhythms of nature through the manipulation of creative materials. The very nature of each different material used will produce a different result—there will be new and unfamiliar inventions of the arms, legs, head and body as you react to the object that you have chosen to work with. Choose your materials carefully—try to decide whether you want the transparency and the airy lightness of plastic, whether you want to react to the texture and shape of wood; the cutting jagged quality of aluminium scrim; the coiling lines of wire.

You might not have very much of an idea to start with, but if you are not indifferent to the individual properties of your material and if you study them in the light of motion and not as a static state, then I think that you will be able to respond to them creatively—working inventively could be a quick spontaneous process or it could be slow and arduous—your ideas, whether abstract or an expression with human overtones, should not float about in your mind but should develop a form so that what you wanted to say from inside yourself will be solved and communicate its meaning to others.

40 Alexander Calder, by James Johnson. The Museum of Modern Art, New York, 1951, p. 70.

Be daring and original, courageous and determined to carry your own idea through. Often the meaning may be clear to you but it does not communicate anything to the spectator. The rest of the class should be able to make suggestions as to how your range of movement may be extended and developed. It may be necessary to rearrange, refine, discard passages of movement invention, so that your original idea remains clear and more effective and the construction more articulate, individual and fresh. This critical analysis of each others work is not aimed to be destructive, but aims at being informed about what to look for and why, so that the creative aspects of what one is trying to build have meaning and expression.

This is in the nature of another dance experience for you—break away from a mechanical manipulation of your prop—and away from the known, safe movements—try to discover your own way of solving this dance problem try to synthesise movement, materials and idea into a satisfying aesthetic unity.

The interplay of design whether symmetry, asymmetry, opposition should be simple and sparse, depending on the nature of the materials used and the idea—there should be an organic unity and vitality in the final form of each construction—not a reproduction of technical movements but a structure that is original—a good beginning with each movement developed from the preceding movement—a sequence of movement enhanced by the inventive manipulation of the materials—nor for mere adornment but to add a new dimension to the movement.

"A small green shoot slowly emerges from mother earth and is born to the world"—(year seven pupil, aged eleven years).

We decided to experiment with contour, as each line that the body makes is the result of a movement—each contour whether straight, curved or broken should relate to other lines of movement. The twisted lines of the arms and legs and intertwining of parts of the body are reminiscent of "a curled leaf" or a "charred log"; bodies tilting sideways appear to be blown by a strong wind in different directions; spiralling movements recapture sets of spirals in flowers.

A changing succession of contours can often quite by accident produce a visual sequence showing the relationship to human motion and nature in a harmonious relationship between a contour and the creative materials.

A changing succession of contours as the hands move in relation to other parts of the body. The hands press slowly downwards so that the shape of the body is like a leaf-stalk; hands undulating at the hips like fish fins; wide contours of the arms and legs as a leg is swung forwards and backwards like a spider throwing out her silken line into space.

Hands can explore the space in the shape of shells—delicate, fragile, articulating from the wrist—the fingers separating successively outwards and inwards like a fan. Clenching and unclenching, hands cupped; tense and spiky fingers like tiger lilies with the backs of the hands touching and hands and fingers circling from the wrists—knuckles bent and hands like claws—BIRD FORMS.

In standing, long rippling back waves with curving contours as the movement unfolds successively through the body, feet, knees, hips, back, chest and head with the arms completing the unfolding—in sitting, successive curling forwards of the back and then the releasing of the back with the opening and closing of hands and arms into delicate and beautiful movement.

83

Some rolled about as stones—from one position to another—taking their weight on their back or on one arm, half twisting from one side to the other; some changed direction and positions incessantly. Knees bent and skittering around the floor in crouched body positions—hands and feet were deliberately placed on the floor and shifted slowly into strange design positions so that the human body was transformed into a primeval shape with the floor as the point of contact. The hollowing out of the body as it assumes rounded forms.

Let your imagination take over, become someone or something else, be aware of the new experience of moving differently. Try to remember the "feel" of that new movement. Develop the courage to create—look around you, be curious about the world; discover the kind of person you are.

If you find yourself imitating someone else's movement do not worry about it—because that movement may give you an idea to build your own movements with your own style or quality. Each time you create something you have experienced artistic growth, and if you have expressed your idea meaningfully to others then you will have taken part in the wonderful experience of communication of an artistic realisation of the imagination through dance.

Every time you start a movement, think of the meaning. Why am I moving in this way? Experience the physical pulls as you move away from what you know into ways of moving that are unfamiliar to you. You are going to need vitality and strength for your creative forms.

Choose materials of today. Plastics, aluminium, brutal materials from the junk-yard; wire and iron.

In your constructions you may wish to recreate the force and angularities of scaffolding—the precariousness of balance—of new angles and contours—new heights, size, colour.

Through the use of the Gesture[41] (the result of a feeling) your coil of wire, or rubber tubing, or wooden fragment will become NOT merely an appendage but an articulate extension of your imaginative forces.

A sincere involvement with your creative process and an absorption with your material and you will evolve a creative form which will convey your meaning and to which we will respond.

For variety and stimulation in solving the creative problems, direct movement phrases into different directions; use asymmetrical and "dissonant"[42] lines of movement to reach outside the serene and orderly lines of symmetry. If you wish to express anxiety, restlessness, or the spirit of man searching for a way out of his dilemma, then use the language of strange and "dissonant movement"[43] of one part of the body pulling against the other—the clash—the jarring of one movement not followed in a predictable unity by another. There, the strong hint of argument, and an acute awareness of the body moving out into unfamiliar directions. For further contrast we need to use the oppositional line—the strongest lines of movement—suggesting protest, aggression, disagreement—conflict.

When we walk we use the opposition of our left arm moving forward against the right leg and then the left arm moves against the right foot as it takes the

41 Doris Humphrey—Tools of Composition.

42 Louis Horst—Composer Music and Modern Dance Forms, U.S.A.

43 Louis Horst.

84

weight—but in the dance the oppositional movement is developed with the use of the opositional lines of the body and its parts. Because they are moving in opposite directions, this produces a tension—when two bodies form lines that move in opposition to each other a strong feeling of resistance is expressed.

The choice of different variations of creative materials was discussed by the class and they decided to work with wood, wire, papier mache, rope and fabric, associating the qualities of these materials with dance expressions. There was a great deal of searching out of opinions among individuals and groups in the class as to the expressive qualities, shapes and creative form that the working materials should assume. There were some students in the class who seemed to have few ideas to contribute and they seemed to readily agree to become part of a group and share ideas and suggestions of others. By working with a group in this way they could enrich their own dance experience. Some of the individuals in the class did not accept the ideas of others and clung to their own creative resolutions. These girls, at times, had a quite unique understanding of the possibilities of the material.

The teacher has to stimulate the child's imagination and not restrict her thinking. The class must have complete freedom to express their opinions and the teacher needs to be aware of the smallest sign from a child that she has something to communicate. Some of the more self-conscious members of the class welcomed the security of working within a group.

To achieve a stimulating atmosphere necessary for a creative form to evolve, a teacher needs a deep insight into her own work, and the topic, and a quick eye to appreciate the efforts of the class—also sensitivity in feeling about the way that a dance-student expresses the topic. She must show a sincere concern for the quality of their artistic experiences and achievements.

Co-operation and respect when listening and watching another group's interpretation. In this way a unity of purpose, communication and an aesthetic ideal is realised through a dance experience. Artistic guidance and growth and the aim for high cultural standards should be part of the environment in which the dance students function.

Nothing shoddy, or meagre or shallow but the kind of work from each individual that will be enriching and "which then reveals and shapes the images, feelings, and emotions of each child".[44]

Above all, your creative forms need the expression of sculptor Jacques Lipchitz, when he was describing the making of his famous bronzes, "with the passion and joy of discovery".

Creative Materials Used:

Wood—(Poles)

Our first work was with wood and the class agreed to work with long poles about 5 to 6 feet in length and shorter wooden rods (broom handles would be suitable). The poles and rods were of varying thicknesses and lengths. Some of the students painted the poles in imaginative contrasting colours and visual

---

44 *Art and Education in Contemporary Culture* by Irving Kaufman. Macmillan Company, New York, 1966; p. 106.

designs. This produced sensations and tensions and created an atmosphere peculiar to the idea or mood.

Blacks and reds created an atmosphere of fierceness.

Greys produced a sombre tone of grief.

The class tested their material in movement. They needed to form impressions and opinions about the character and expressive possibility of their prop.

"Inflexible"

"Few expressive qualities"

"Difficult to shape"

"Taut"

"No delicacy or grace"

I watched the human figures move about, combining their poles or rods with dance movement.

Shapes, directions changed with a design relationship emerging between body movement and their wooden props.

Relationships began to develop as poles were thrust towards a focal point— rods fanned outwards like spokes of a wheel—rise and fall, combinations of levels and lengths forming a rhythmic shape in the space.

Poles were moved into oblique or diagonal lines or formed parallel lines as they were held by two or more people. The length of the line was extended by bending movements of the body, or a leg that was extended front or back.

A moving kaleidoscope of four figures moved successively (one after the other) into different levels exploring directions from the four corners and through high, middle and low points. They shifted their positions constantly using the three dimensions, giving an impression of impermanence and change.

The poles were held by students at each of the ends and both were connected and lines interacted and angles stressed. The design narrowed until poles and figures were shaped like a Gothic spire—vertically pointing heavenward; bodies stretched outward and extended their wooden frames outward like a giant hand.

Other groups shifted into diverse relationships with the centre of the constructions continually changing, and the focus of the movement shifting up or down or from side to side. Movement changed rhythmically as the form changed and developed. There were balanced symmetrical designs, an even placement of figures and objects—other movement-forms showed the tensions of oppositional pulls between figures and the creative materials.

Intent at first on a known geometric relationship, the class later shaped their constructions with more stress on the unknown.

Construction, design and appearance of the shapes became more free; investigation by the class of a more creative approach to their materials intensified; reactions to thicknesses, lengths, colours, lines and angles and the

Constructions: Poles
Photograph: Robert Walker

projection of the designs into space were expressed through an imaginative language of movement. The interest aroused among the dance students, by the constant manipulation of their material, led the class to relate their objects to mature and man-made shapes.

Poles could become expressive and communicate:

". . . a spear . . . a hunter."

". . . the energetic abstraction of a road sign."

". . . biblical, divine . . . a Rod."

". . . stake—martyrs, crucifiixion . . . medieval."

"the compartment-like designs of modern buildings."

"Japanese sword fight."

"a stave . . . a crook."

"attack and defence . . ."

"aggression."

"Totemic emblem."

"The rituals of folk lore."

"A blade of grass."

In our discussion groups, we found that within the "rigid framework" of the pole there still existed a pliable outlet for themes and ideas—that it should not be merely an exercise based on design alone, but there should be a connection between idea, the creative material and the dance language. The compositions could comment on and relate to people, things and events around them; expressing feelings and emotions about the world we live in.

The group illustrated this by forming a cage of wooden rods. Some were held vertically, or balanced along the back of their necks—they entwined their arms around the wood.

The cage dominated the hunted figure who was imprisoned in the structure. The hunter stalked behind it with long cat-like walks and springs as it was being pushed and pounded across the floor.

The animal awakens, so does the hunter—

The hunter stalks the gentle animal. In one hand a spear, in the other the dreaded cage.

Margaret—*year seven.*

"Run—to escape—too late.

The hunter has caught sight of you . . .

The animal hates the being that imprisons it.

It must kill or be killed

     Kill or be killed

     Kill—killed

     Kill

        Kill

          Kill

            Kill"

Ropes *(Ann, year ten)*

"A rope—in semblance, but inside a fiery, inextinguishable spirit, eager to entangle and entwine, slithering around the human body like a snake."

        Surrender

        Snarl

        Snake

        Ships

        Theseus and the Minotaur

        Captivity

        Cowboy

        Strangle

        Whirlpool

        The curve of a suspension bridge

Rope Variations
Photographs: Robert Walker
Opposite photograph:
Denise Fletcher

Ropes were of different thicknesses and textures—rough and smooth—wiry —coarse, heavy—fine, light, and narrow, thick.

The material was cut into different lengths depending on the number of individuals in a group, and according to the idea—

There were variations in colour—white ropes, effective red ropes, restful blue, severe black ropes and emerald green.

Discover how far you can develop your material.
—Texture, lengths, shapes, colours.
"Create with your ropes over smooth stretched surfaces."[45]
Lines were straight and described by the class as vital, severe—
—If the lines were horizontal then the feeling of the structure was more reposeful (no conflicting twisted ropes).
—the vertical line seemed narrow and direct.
—If all the sides of the structures were jointed, the spatial areas seemed closed or imprisoned.
—The stretched surfaces seemed to connect the tension between the figures—
As the ropes were traced out from one dance student to the next, the lines stretched out into many diverse directions.
As you manipulate the ropes, think in terms of texture, weight, flexibility, tension and release of tension.
Straight lines were accurately measured with dance movement in the shape of a square, rectangle, triangle and pentagon, with five sides. These designs were purely geometric with no emotive qualities whatsoever.
Try to construct as many designs as possible—and resolve your design from perhaps a four-sided figure to a three-sided figure passing through a curve.
There should be a feeling of continuity in the designs and an awareness between rope, the position of the body and the ground; the feeling of space in, around and through the structures; the sudden changes in direction which will bring new visual effects, the change in the organisation of space with areas contracting or expanding with a sense of the third dimension. These are all aspects for your consideration as you train your "eye" to appreciate the line.
If you wish to change your rhythmic energies break out of the bold straight lines and rigid angularities and express yourselves with the creative material through the continuations of curves.
The class experimented with movements of the curved line, using both the body and the ropes. The rhythmic energies changed in accordance with the choice of lines or design of the dance movement—there was more suppleness and lyricism, less rigidity and direct thrusts—less straight extensions of the legs, arms or the body—the lines developed into sweeping curves; the curve of the leg, the rounded arms, movement in the curve of the back continued through into the cradle-like suspension of the ropes.
To convey to us a sensation that was weightless and illusive, the ropes were looped, swinging freely in arcs, achieving an expression of effortless grace.

45 Lynden Dadswell—Sculptor, Australiaa

The eye should sweep across the motion of the gentle curve of rope, extended by the curved lines of the dance movements—static, or successive, or broken curves, the indication of the curve, or the free-swinging curvi-linear designs.

The modern dance vocabulary which has its origin in the flowing curved line, or arc of the contraction—release technique, is ideal for this harmonious line.

For instance, the circles of the body with the weight on both knees or one knee, and the arms describing a circle; or successively (one after the other); outward or inward circles of the arms; the body waves—forward, back and side; the side and back bends; the pelvic contractions and side contractions; the curves around the back; the leg circles out and in; the forward developpé with a back bend.

The unity of these circular movements with the rope designs make an expressive overall form in which no single part would be complete if it were separated from the whole. The formation of a shape can evolve from some simple movement and the form grows as the patterns progress.

The groups can now begin to vary the curved lines; curvilinear shapes begin to unfold with the flow of lines, moving freely or sustained.

If you wish to create a transparent effect, then devise your structure with the air flowing freely around and through the rope construction.

A puzzling and disturbing effect is achieved by twisting and spiralling all your ropes so that there is a writhing of materials. Curvilineal and rectilineal designs can be combined and groups can organise the interplay of ropes to express tenuous, delicate and light sensations, moving with changing timing elements. The forceful oppositional pulls—the dynamic energy through the use of diagonals. The cluster of converging lines focus energies inward while another group releases the ropes from a central figure outward and so the tensions flow out to the extremities of the space

The creative effort should have intention. Is the design of primary importance or is a human element expressed in the form with emotional significance? You (the teacher) and the class will have to decide this question.

Each individual's reaction to the inventions could be different and vary widely, depending on personal interpretation and the angle at which one sees the structure—there should be a changing, moving design. These space structures are best viewed "in the round".

Everything is shifting—
The taut lines of a triangular shape are eased into graceful curves; the dance student executes a slow back fall and the ropes loosen from her arms—each loop is lifted off and used by others as separate circles.

Groups connect their space structures and there is an intensifying of creativity as ropes carry stretched and curved surfaces into new directions.

They cross, intersect, bisect, to form an intricate design with the floor as the focal point; or ropes carrying tension above floor level and lines extending upward into a column. The fascinating patterns are controlled by the dance movements of the body. On the floor, on the knees, falling to the floor; moving across the floor twisting to the floor; rotating, bending, extending and flexing in a pattern of ever-changing movements merging with the rope designs into an integrated whole.

To give more dextrous invention connect the ropes to different parts of the body—ingeniously linking rope ends to toes, curving around the ankle or wind and twine the creative materials around arms and legs. Each girl should try to be aware of what her partner or group-dancers are doing. Aware of the detail of the design and its variations—aware of the surfaces and the transparencies—of the change and growth of the design—control and manipulation of the dance movement with the creative materials.

One needs to be able to wander freely among the constructions; actually walking or crawling through the forms so that one can connect with the dimensions—appreciating from inside, rather than a one-sided external recognition of the form. Some dance-students linked their rope designs to others so that there would be an expanding of expressive forms. Three dimensional linking with flat two-dimensional designs; oppositional tensions linking with passive symmetrical designs; dance figures connected by oblique and curved ropes moved across the floor like the sails of a ship, the pulls between them were at times taut and resisting, then free and relaxed.

A loose design was spread out on the floor—an island—one dance figure moved within its confines in a melancholy way.

Ropes hung down from the shoulders—a cloak. The image of a cradle as she linked rope ends to her hands and feet.

Ropes were unravelled across the floor, figures ran or leapt spontaneously— a busy, active scene.

A web of ropes and the group figures surged forward and enmeshed one of the group into the interpenetration of their vibrant, quivering maze.

By now years nine and ten classes had learned to work on the creative dance problem. They had gradually learned to suggest and to accept ideas from others. They had experimented with ways to express themselves, releasing their imagination. Some reacted quickly to this and others were more reticent and slow to change.

The dance students found the atmosphere enjoyable and stimulating and this helped them to create with confidence and to enlighten and acquaint others with the qualities of their individual creative piece.

Wire

We wanted to shape the wire suggesting movement in space describing flow, twists, rhythms, texture.

Size and proportion had to be carefully worked out with the constructions related to the human figure and to dance movement.
"Flexible"
"Wire can be bent, twisted, hollowed out"
The movement of the sculptures indicated shapes;

       circle

       square

cylindrical

pyramid

spirals

free form

There were certain filled-in spaces of the wire forms. These were of papier-mache and the inventions were fearless, rich and exploratory.

Total constructions were painted pale colours like a soap bubble; some were in hard colours. To create a phantom landscape—thick projections like roots extended outward from a central form—the child's impression of trees.

Most wire constructions remained in a fixed shape but one group kept changing the form to suit the expression of their creative thoughts and fantasies in relation to the world around them. The curving wire shape was expanded as the idea took shape, bent, twisted, coiled and new spaces were formed for the human bodies to move through. The wire was manipulated according to the development of the expressive themes.

Some constructions were made as separate units and fitted together at random—this produced different meanings—a maze; umbrellas; series of birds or boxes; the expression of his or her imagination. The constructions were completed quickly always in the dance lessons, while the ideas were fresh in their minds. There was a growing realisation of the variety of ways that a figure could move in and with the constructions. The rhythmic designs of movements had to find their counterpart in the manipulation of the wire forms.

There was constant change and motion as the body and its parts invented patterns, in particular the arms and legs moved expressively; through the space across the floor, and into the air. Threading arms and legs through the open spaces into shapes; climbing over and through the shapes; balances as if perched upon scaffolding; the expressive forces, the designs of movement, the unity of the purpose of the wire shapes with movement, all motivated by the idea, produced certain gestures and influenced the shapes and the way the groups handled them. This creative activity expressing the students' world of experience continued to be fertile, exploring the spatial and directional possibilities of their creative problem; discarding as far as they were able their inhibitions and feelings of inadequacy and set conventional attitudes, and responding to the experiment in a new way—altering and shaping their movement to produce the effect needed for their images—contours distorted, reflecting alarm, horror, panic, discontent or symmetry and unison providing the desired communication of peace, serenity, resignation.

*   *   *

Group Sculpture in Wire and Dance Movement

Margaret's Group (year ten, average age 15 years)

We used the overall shape of a CONE.

We filled in some of the wire spaces representing the Being that blocked out the sunlight of Freedom.

The open spaces represented the emptiness of life—the boredom of nothing-ness—

We extended the wire—curved and twisted corners and shaped it rhythmi-cally until we had an intricately shaped cage. Our colours were greys and blues, and matched the heartless way in which the human spirit could be imprisoned. Our cage was light and easy to handle with spaces large enough to move about in.

The tense and short movements of the victim as she realised the restrictions of her freedom—the strange pulls of the body expressing frustration.

—Terror as the victim tossed about in the wire sculpture.

—Forceful pushes suggesting aggression and turbulence.

—The cage becomes a weapon. Arms and legs twisted and were thrust out of the cage. The dynamic pulsations of the contraction or impulses of the body increased in an attempt to become free. At the end, the movements fused with the distorted planes of the wire and webs of the construction.

Bella's Group:

Black and white.

Black . . . death, . . . the responsibility of degeneration . . . Black blobs.

White . . . Life . . . innocence . . . purity . . . happiness.

The group formed a honeycomb of figures—symbolising our sculpture. The black figures were grim and moved in a repetitious way in patterns across the floor—the arms and legs moved mechanically—stiffly and jerkily with strange isolations of the flexed foot, head and arms and legs, moving in circles up and down or side to side.

The white figures of innocence were serene using symmetrical and parallel dance movement.

Between each group there was a feeling of tension as the wire construction is moved slowly to and fro between the resisting groups—one group trying to overcome the other—until they mingle, forming a rigid circular formation attempting to hem each other in—all clustered around the cage which forms the centre and almost submerged by this inflexible group.

Jillian's Group:

A place of peace and safety—somewhere to rest before we emerge into the world—A Cocoon.

96

Our movement is harmonious, rounded, nothing harsh as we lay curled up inside our sculpture.

It flowed with whorls of wire to create a design of continuous curves so that each person could enter and curl up and slowly revolve.

The wires were a series of spirals all joined like a caterpillar.

Our movement extended and curled inwards and spiraled along the floor revolving in our shell like the larva of an insect, the figure inside the cocoon moved continuously, expressing the movement of life.

Helen's Group:

At the twist of your wrists you are off—Propellers spin.

You are swirling through space. Sometimes high—sometimes low—legs become propellers—circling inwards and outwards—you are a gyrating, twisting shape.

Slow down—an arm circles a leg, extends horizontally. The body and head are released forwards; your house is still whirring on your back.

You are the centre of the circling machine.

Rosemary's Sculpture:

You walk cautiously and touch the thread that connects two worlds.

The brilliant landscape of one world attracts you.

You put on the circular disc—it is deceptive.

Your powers of invention are started and you give birth to a whole new series of movements.

You wind the disc around you—your body—your arm—you curl it around your hand, you balance it on your foot—you rotate the disc and curve in many directions—the movements become faster as you bend and revolve and spin within this world. The pace increases until it becomes too free, maddening, incomprehensible, uncontrollable, flung out—

Impossible to stop!

Fabric

Inspired by Lola's writing, her group in year nine, decided to dance the theme of fire using material and paint. They were fresh and original in their approach and they dyed several yards of fabric on which were painted colourful designs which seemed to leap about.

The colours emphasised hues of flame and fire and sunsets—yellow and orange—clashing reds evoked frenzy—unusual black forms emphasised the doom of a charred landscape.

97

Scarf
Photograph: Kay E. Martin

"Fire suggests mystery. There are red hot colours and leaping yellow flames. Sweat and perspiration gather in great lumps. Stinging winds howl. Red hot embers smother while cruel colours jump about. The balls of fire leap from tree to tree, bush to grass, to dry leaves.

"A blood-red sun overlooks the blaze. Heat rises, while curves, red and yellow, dart about in quick movements.

"You fight but you are weak against the force—the raven flies overhead. The fire is here. You are alight—all of you—you are fire."[46]

The several points of view of the dancers in the group as to how to relate to the material and dance movement often gave rise to heated discussions.

The groups had to look creatively at the theme—to fully understand the ideas and feelings behind the words and express them with their technique, and create a continuity of purpose with the use of the material.

46 Lola's creative description.

Fabric
Photograph : Robert Walker

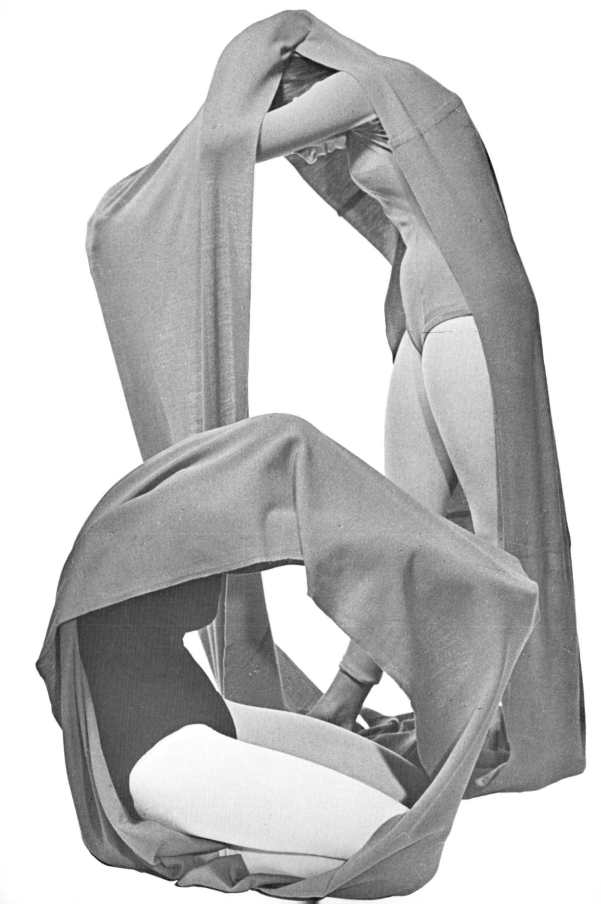

They wanted to communicate the feel of heat, the crackling and sizzling of fire—the spontaneous bursts of energy—the smouldering weirdness.

The group of seven started in the centre moving together in the very smallest way—then they extended outward along various designed paths. They found it necessary to make their designs clear and the unfolding of these surfaces were danced at a variety of levels. The floor pattern consisted of diagonals, zig-zags and small circles.

The directions that the dancer took were unexpected; sharp and sudden turns, one figure moving behind another—

The moving floor pattern gave us the impression of a changeable, shifting scene.

Jumps and leaps with flexed feet punctuated the vibratory movements.

The combination of the group changed.

Five against two—one, two, three, one.

Now the figures turned in spirals—curving the body as the leg is circled, stretched or bent inwards or outwards; or one figure circling her arm and another figure circling the leg.

The circles of the body and the spiral turns produced an effect of wisps of curling smoke.

With the movement there was an interplay of undulating, rotating, spiralling material—a vast curtain of red billowing silk.

The mass of cloth was handled with ingenuity, starting in a crumpled heap, a nucleus, a spark, it emerged as a moving shape, an interplay between movement and dancers.

It rippled, was flung out into space, and traced out moving, crimson streams along the floor.

The movement was asymmetrical, designed to show the excitement of red, the agitation, the effervescence, the danger. There was a restlessness in the changing floor pattern, and jumps which were tense, with the body or parts of the body pointing or turned away from the centre.

The tensions increased as the dancers drew closer and the invisible pulls of purpose, motive, design, connected one to the other.

The red cloth covered them. Increased pulsations by the group as they breathed in and out set this burning mound in motion again.

A delicate rhythm as the shape flowed to and fro.

More turbulence of heat as figures moved forcefully up and down. Sharper, pointed movements of fingers, arms, elbows, knees accented upwards into the canopy-like crackling sparks. Finally, the whole form pulsating and vibrating with sharp and strong movement, as the flames leapt higher until the material was thrown high into the air, exploded, and the figures took their shape out of their environment—dissolving into twisted, distorted, inharmonious figures—transforming their landscape into a silent wasteland.

A group of dance students commented on Margaret's[47] attempt to capture and express all that she knew about an object—she proposed to show them on every plane how a lifeless object could be transformed into an animated and expressive dimension for dance.

47 Margaret, a year ten dance student, and member of Fort Street Dance Group.

Margaret encased herself in a tube of stretch jersey material—which became the frame for the whole outward shape. At first she worked in the space at high levels and then she gravitated to floor level.

The lines could be extended to the fullest because the jersey could stretch with the body upward and outward in horizontal and vertical lines.

The two-dimensional pulls were flat and precise—

The jersey was usually taut and stretched and as Margaret moved inside symmetrically so did the outward shape take similar equal lines.

At times different changes of weight and curves and twists wove the jersey into deep folds like waves. For some time she invented with verticals and sharp diagonals and she looked like—a pillar—a peak. At one stage at floor level she was lying completely covered by the jersey—she looked like—a smooth stone—an embryo—she was motionless.

Then the human form exerted itself again—the torso twisted this way and that.

The dimension and texture changed from large—to heavy—to thick—to soft—to small—and knees, elbows and fingers were, at times, pinnacles.

Margaret was fully stretched on the floor on her back—one leg extended vertically. She appeared like a boat; her outstretched body along the floor formed the boat shape and the material over her upward and outward stretched arms formed a smooth triangular sail. Her flexed foot formed the apex. The whole form was completely encased. The cloth without the moving human form was lifeless—a piece of jersey lying on the floor was uncommunicative but the motions of the body from within gave to Margaret and to us a sense of the sculptural form OF THE BODY IN ACTION.

Chairs *Photograph: Denise Fletcher*

Chairs

"Now no longer substance

No longer wielded from the carpenter's tool

The angle is gone

The rigid steel that bound it

And the very conception of its existence

Gone—for a moment of ETERNITY—to real things.

Real for the deepest of intellect,

For the highest of philosophy.
The material line, the form and weight,

No longer wielded from the carpenter's tool
But a tool for the art to wield.

And the ARTIST

He too the change has undergone.

We see him with more than just our eye,

We hear his breath with more than just our ear

What he represents is more than just the executioner.

And if, for a second, the eternity is broken

And he lapses from it—

The emotion is found in someone standing by,

The onlooker, who feels the call, finds a wisp

Of the thread and is carried for ever on it—

For there is no knot nor union there upon it."

Hadie (year eleven; aged sixteen years)

This work for three dance students was characterised by its dramatic content, as the trio lavished their attention on three chairs which became symbols of possessiveness, fear, hate and greed.

The composition was stimulated by the compelling experimental score by Alwin Nikolais.[48] The chairs evoked a distinctive reaction among the trio and there were a series of three duets which finally turned into a labyrinth of transient relationships and erupting emotional atmosphere.

The first girl curved in and around the circular frame of her chair—she pursued it with soft, melancholy movements and became so engrossed in what

48 Modern Dance Choreographer—U.S.A.

she was doing that she seemed to be able to mould the movements with the chair to exactly suit the mood that she wanted to express.

Finally (and this happened quite by chance) the circular seat of the chair fell out, and she used it as a disc—curving back with it, diving downwards, twisting with it like a huge moon.

The second duet was full of energetic spontaneity with leaps and balances. This gave one the feeling of an encounter, as one girl used the chair in a series of positive vital movements affirming her mastery over her opponent.

The third invention, found in the stiff-backed chair, a symbol for aggression and flashes of unyielding moods. A series of actions developed as the aggressive one resolved to capture all the possessions. There was an air of urgency as she set forth to defeat her opponents—strutting pompously from one to the other

The trio tugged and pulled—the chairs became machines as they were driven across the floor.

The melancholy one crawled away, seized the disc, and gave herself up with the utmost speed to dynamic falls and flowing figures of eights, of arms and legs. She lost interest in her chair and with a whirling action fell and paused, curving protectively around the disc

A gesture of possession and the aggressive one piled the chairs into her own corner. She had to cover the space in all directions, returning constantly to guard her pile. At times she had to retrieve a chair that had been taken from the heap by the energetic and purposeful one.

The aggressive figure hunted her down, dragged her on to the heap of chairs and imprisoned her in the framework.

The final strutting triumph of the victorious one as she climbed animatedly over her possessions.

The trio was concerned at first with discovering the potential of their movement with the chairs through an improvisational approach. Time and time again this task drew upon the young student's imagination, and inventiveness. It took a lot of work, and criticism and questions before we could find the right way of expressing the imagination with these props.

The movements had to "feel" right; and the experiences that grew out of the situation with the chairs and the changing relationship with each of the students had to have meaning. Each time we improvised something quite new and different was created.

The group decided to keep the best movement experiences and drop those aspects of the dance that did not communicate anything; that was in any way just an automatic movement no matter how well executed.

They chose chairs as being part of their environment; easily moveable and the best objects that would lend themselves to becoming an expressive extension of their personalities and behaviour. After expressing their idea through spontaneous movement improvisation we selected a sequence of actions with dramatic gestures.

The composition then began to take shape and we rehearsed it for quite a long period until the physical technique was well done, and we were content that the emotional intensity and the unpredictable inter-relationships between figures and chairs were relevant and inspiring to those dancing and to those watching.

A shortened version of The Chairs was filmed in 1965 by the Commonwealth Film Unit as part of Australian Diary 133[49] released in cinemas in Australia and abroad.

---

49 This choreosonic score by Alwin Nikolais, American modern dance choreographer, was released to us for the accompaniment of the modern dance work—"The Chairs".

11 SYMPHONY FOR IMPROVISERS

The time for improvisation is a time to develop
something of one's own, to discover new forms,
and to free the imagination—working alone or
with others, self-reliant, and with originality
and quality, breeding the elements of discovery.

"A need: an anguish, a restlessness, a buzzing:
something is deeply moved in us: there is an
uneasy disturbing throbbing: we feel the need
to create."[50]

50 Create! page 299, from *Foundations of Modern Art* by Ozenfant (Dover Publications, New York).

New dance movements born out of the creative talent of the individual need the opportunity to be expressed.

Finding ways of making the imagination visible through movement of the human body—one movement linked to the next, one discovery following another and so the gradual evolution of countless extraordinary and fascinating shapes.

The capacities (emotional, imaginative, intellectual), of each individual and her own personal experience can find an outlet through movement quickened by the stimulation of improvisation. Yet each student is limited by her own technical deficiencies and often wants to express themes which are too ambitious. The expression of dramatic themes, if the technique is inadequate and creative experimentation immature, will only give the individual a sense of frustration and insecurity—however, if the student cannot express creative ideas with satisfying bodily movement, this consciousness often spurs her on to improve technical capacities and to continue the search for more expressive and imaginative movement.

The interplay of one dance movement with another—the active and never-ending process of original, spontaneous movement through dance improvisation, linking movements with those of others, until dance relationships are discovered. Through the creative processes involved in the improvisation,

Improvisations
Photography: Anthony Horth

different designs between figures, different uses of space, of rhythm, qualities of feeling and meaning in an imaginative theme, can interest and absorb the young dance student. The improvisational approach need not necessarily lead to dance composition but the viewpoint of Doris Humphrey,[51] American choreographer, was that creative improvisation should be started as soon as possible because it extended the student's ability, skill and imagination to create.

The creative dance experience should be available to all children, from the earliest school years through to College and University and need not necessarily be the province of the professional dancer. In every individual's life, the creative dance experience should be given an opportunity to be expressed through the discovery of the dance as a means of expression, a projection through movement of their own personality, and to deepen awareness of the inherent possibilities of the world around them.

This can lead to a fuller understanding of the other arts; fine arts, music, drama, aesthetics, literature. The responsibility of the teacher is to guide and encourage the dance student towards artistic growth by introducing them to some of the aspects of other arts and their relation and interaction on the dance and to each other—encouragement to identify with nature. The world of oceanic life, of plants and animals—their colours, habits, shapes, and means of locomotion—the rhythmic undulations of the sea—the texture of sand and the dynamics of the volcano.

The kingdom of insects and their predatory and protective devices. The co-ordination of the curves in geometry, with the curved lines in movement design.

One must create the right atmosphere for the improviser—a sense of freedom; time and space for creating. The working atmosphere needs a quiet sympathetic environment; free from noise, laughter or ridicule or any destructive element which will inhibit the individual; yet with a sense of enjoyment as the young dancer begins to unfold her movements in the voyage of discovery.

What thoughts are in the minds of the Improviser?
"Do they have a theme?"
"Are they really involved in finding new ways of moving the body, or are their movements false?"
"Are the Improvisers prepared to leave the security of the floor?"

We see the figures moving out into the space.

Among the inexperienced, improvisation at first is probably best kept at a level of experience suited to the individual—the studies, not too long, so that each excursion into movement discovery, does not lose meaning or become repetitious.

This movement improvisation needs involvement purely for its own sake— irrespective of standard of technique or knowledge of the modern dance vocabulary. You begin to move and you never know where that first movement

51 Studies and Discussions with Miss Humphrey on the Creative Process, U.S.A. 1958, 59, 60.

will lead you. Selfconsciousness gradually slips away if you take courage and start to involve yourself in what you are doing. Here is scope for the imagination to be released into movement.

As the students develop their intellectual curiosity and their creative dance vocabulary, and the wherewithal to present it is broadened, by selecting and discarding wisely, then the improvisational experience can be lengthened in time and themes.

Improvisational compositions are a logical step among a group who are dance-educated enough to react to stimuli (space, time, group relationships, percussion, voice, areas of sound, areas of music), seeing line, quality and meaning in the movements.

They are able to evolve a compositional form, germinating from improvisational material and movements of the group, and their relationship one to the other and to the space.

Their readiness to see the implications in the situation and capture them in movement. The form grows with the moulding of the improvisational materials until a composition has evolved—this can be repeated, and the work can be enduring but not always with the same succession of movement sequences. Parts of the improvised compositional unit can remain intact and co-ordinated, while other connections through the composition change and rely on improvised individual and group dance movement, with sudden unpremeditated innovations.

Each improvisational project is a new experiment created each time with a fresh approach, becoming more and more selective, in discarding that which has no quality or meaning—that which is artificial, banal, does not excite, move or communicate its meassage to the spectator.

The work should have insight. The creative process is at times painful and laborious, but those who have something to say, will continue to assert themselves and be willing to participate in the discovery of the unknown.

Those who give up, believing that they have nothing creative to add and are content to become "the watchers" need sympathetic recognition of their feelings and abilities as well as tolerance and encouragement at the slightest emergence of creative thought or action.

One must not be afraid to become acquainted with the way one's own body can move—the hollow and linear formations, the fluidity, the hardness, the flexibility, the tenuous threads, the energy, joy and passion in movement—the delicate balances, the expressive power of muscular and explosive energy, all contributing to the creative potential in the creator, giving expression to an active, non-verbal statement of fertile dance-forms.

The improvisor develops an instinctive selection for expressive dance material and a keen knowledge of the movement-sensation; responding to a movement that is "right"—"It feels right" the discovery that one moves quite differently from any other person. That each movement has a distinct and unique value of its own.

The concern of the teacher for the creative efforts, understanding, encouragement, respect and sympathy for the student's creative contribution and intention adds greatly to the success or failure of the project. A sincere appraisal by the teacher of efforts, however tentative, and apparently insignificant, should contribute to the confidence of the student. The teacher must give the students courage to overcome their frustrations, and inspire them to release their creative potential. This needs tenacity and patience, continuity and conviction by the teacher for the creative growth of the individual spirit.

The climate that is set by the teacher for communication, must be a sensitive one—an understanding of the opinions of the class; providing the individual with an opportunity to contribute to the action, in the light of their own experience. The students need to feel free to express themselves, need to know what is going on, and what to look for. Opinions should be encouraged and the environment and methods changed if the results of a project are disappointing. The atmosphere needs to be flexible with suggestions and corrections by the teacher when disparities occur between independent expressive individuals in the class, and those who are inhibited in their creative experiments.

* * *

A Flight of Fantasies

The world of fantasy offers one rich material for dance studies and creative dance themes. If you expect to discover in yourself the power of fantasy so that you can portray and reflect certain characteristics of mankind in a fanciful way, then your ideas, studies and descriptions must be imaginative.

You can people your world with mystical characters, fairy-stories and miraculous feats. In fanciful movement, one needs light irregular coquettish gestures and certain distortion of movement. The bizarre or grotesque is evident in the contrasts and incongruities of movement.

Our creative power lies in the use of the imagination. It is in our power to keep our sense of wonder and delight alive in ourselves and share it with others. We need to constantly re-affirm our creative vision and imaginative faculties by forming new conceptions of persons or things. We need to conceive and shape new images, new ideas, new story-lines—and we need to find new interpretations or connections with events that we actually have experienced, or with an emotional quality that we might relive. Not least, *continually* expand the scope of your reading.

Look with a poet's insight into the fairy tale work of Rackham.[52]

Through his entrancing illustrations of children's literature with poetic and rhythmic language, he brings alive his drawings of human and half-human and non-human creatures and he draws us into his fairy-tale world of atmosphere and texture of forests and trees; wizardry and dragons and giants; floating tresses; purple and silver wings and fairies sewing leaves.

Study the movement and behaviour of animals and insects in King Solomon's Ring.[53] You will find something to dance about in their battles and loves.

52 Arthur Rackham—artist and illustrator.

53 *King Solomon's Ring* by Konrad Z. Lorenz.

The mystery of the Life of the Bee[54] and the Life of the Ant[55] are described with much sensitivity and wisdom by Maeterlinck. He intermingles science and philosophy and fancy.

The curious characters\ in Alice's Adventures Underground[56] and the whimsical drawings by Tenniel should stir your memory of movement for an exercise in the qualities of the fantastic.

Imagine the enrichment of the senses when one is free to dream of the long bindings of silken cloth,[57] gold and red saris, eye of rubies and turquoises, brooches of silver and pearls, grandeur of the Arabian Nights[58]—search for an expressive form which can turn the most mundane and mediocre work into one of perfect balance; of harmony, texture, mood and movement, expressive of human feelings.

More impressions in colour in the Feast of the Seasons, mermaids and castles, dragons and knights[59]—movements are fleeting, changing and fragmented. The grey spirit of the "Great Willow"[60] the feeling of earth, spirits from the first age!

We can find inspiration in the works of Edward Lear.[61] In Daddy Long Legs and the Fly, we can associate his words with movement. There is contrast between the stark stretched movements of the spider and the rapid twitching made by the fly. There is contrast in the rhythmic movement suggesting different characteristics. The ludicrous shapes suggest to us that they are misfits and so the movement leads to some awkwardness, some little imbalance in the composition and quick changes of dynamics.

Our individual sense of delight and awe is aroused and we are always in their debt.

*   *   *

For example my year nine class decided to sit in a circle around the improvisors for "Flight of Fantasies", so that they could see the creative workings as a three-dimensional action, so increasing the depth and variety of the scene.

We set up a workshop log committee[62] who wrote up the creative projects. These were students from the class who later recorded the projects with a description of ideas, comments, thoughts and feelings.

54 The Life of the Bee, choreography—Doris Humphrey.

55 The Ants. Scene from dance work "The Insects", choreography—Gertrud Bodenwieser.

56 *Alice's Adventures Underground* by Lewis Carroll. Illustrations—John Tenniel.

57 *The Silk Road*—L. Boulnois

58 From the *Travels of Marco Polo*—translated by Ronald Latham.

59 Brian Wildsmith—illustrator.

60 *The Lord of the Rings*—J. R. R. Tolkien.

61 Nonsense songs—The Daddy Long Legs and The Fly, by Edward Lear.

62 The following were dance experiences from years Nine, Ten, and Eleven. Average age fourteen, fifteen, and sixteen years.

Before the improvisation, we often discussed again the resources for working spontaneously—one should not rely on the same old ways of moving—one must forget oneself and become seriously absorbed in the action. No distractions—no skimming—avoid the obvious in movement.

We all agreed that our outlets for creativity have narrowed since early childhood.

The frozen flight of movement in "statues"; the creations of our "dressing up" fantasies; rain on cobwebs; the breathless excitement of the make-believe world; tossed about in the memory of a dream.

*   *   *

Water

"free

floating

rippling

rain slashing

drowning

the crescendo of waterfalls

floods engulfing, destruction

rivers like veins in the human body

rocked in a cradle of water,

thirst and drought

bubbling

to Lull."

The class worked in groups responding to the topic that they had chosen. They tried to express their opinion about water in a creative form—trying to communicate to us the quality of water. The groups thought about water and all its associations before they started.

When they were ready they began to move.

Some of them moved with a fluid flow; spontaneous. Others shifted restlessly, trying to capture the wavering motion of water.

There was a growing agitation in the movements of some, suggesting approaching disaster.

Comments:
"We would like to have seen more combinations of arms and legs—not enough excitement in movement."

"The circular motion of the body was expressive of the fluidity of water—"
"Use filmy material across the floor and move it gently to give the impression of water—move with it—little ripples."

"Not too many static poses but an unfolding of body movement and a constant change in movements from up to down."

The groups felt that the topic was a little unreal; that the poetic and delicate qualities of water were harder to express than the forceful strength of movement needed for a flood. One viewpoint was "that the serenity and restlessness were like man's life—the struggle for independence and freedom followed by periods of calm and immobility".

Margaret from year eleven, who has the expressive capacity for creating spontaneously, expanded this impression in her improvisation—she started with slow rippling pulsating hand movements offset by serene symmetrical kneeling positions, then burst forth into swirling falls, and rolls on the floor, dramatising the struggle of man by percussive angular movements of arms and legs using mainly oppositional lines in a combination of fierce activity.

The class comments showed an understanding of the creative requirements of the topic.

"More use of the breath in the movements expressing the qualities and rhythms of water" (movements based on the use of the breath rhythm—even and uneven, broken and unbroken, long and short).

This improvisational situation was significant for its artistic response by the working groups.

When you are no longer involved, and you have nothing more to say, then it is wise to stop your improvisation.

Qualities began to make themselves felt through the creative movement, activities in which gesture, contrast, change of direction and dimension, increased the interesting relationship between the movements.

Be enterprising in your improvisation. Let it grow, develop, and change—finish when the idea has been resolved.

Mirror Images

Image, symbol, likeness, resemblance, imitation, shadow, replica, echo, reprint, caricature, cartoon, impersonation, mimic, mockery.

The idea of the mirror used in literature, as in "Narcissus" of Greek mythology, who fell in love with his own reflection—or "The Birthday of the Infanta"—(the dwarf sees his ugly misshapen likeness in the mirror and dies of grief), from Oscar Wilde's Fairy Stories; "Mirror, mirror, on the wall, who is the fairest of us all", the wicked queen in the fairy story "Snow White".

The girls choose a partner and one mirrors the movements of the other. *The leader* has a completely free choice in deciding what movements she will make and in what direction she will move. The one *following* needs to watch the movements of the leader very carefully. She must work with concentration and be sensitively aware of lines and sudden changes of movement. She should become a perfect replica, observing keenly and following precisely. The leader and the follower need to develop a rapport between them—one conscious of the other.

The one following can also develop a sense of satisfaction—move in a new way. The timing of the movements will be different—the sequences of movements will be quite new—in fact the entire mirror-reflection study will be new dance material; different from anything done before.

Comments by class member

"It is a challenge to work with a partner, whose movements you do not know."

"You should have a chance to become both leader and follower."

"The inventor will realise that not all movement is necessarily well reproduced by others. The standards of technique may be unequal, and movements which suit one body may not suit another."

"The leader was aware of the one who was reproducing her movements—but another leader created only for herself and did not think about her partner's capacity."

As the dance students become more adept at following and building movements using total or partial body movement, they should strive for variation such as percussive movements—sustained or alternate or short and sharp or flowing movements.

Creative efforts can be directed also towards rhythmic complexities in the dance. First, a simple pattern for small groups in a circle. A clearly defined foot rhythm, followed by a turn, a change in direction or level. Each figure reproducing the rhythm and adding her own creative rhythm at the end.

This ability of the instrument (the body) to reproduce a movement or series of movements gives the individual a facility for picking up movements quickly; acquiring a "good eye" for adopting positions, skill in learning rhythmic patterns, recognition of the qualities of a movement, a measure of originality and resourcefulness in contributing one's own creative material, and memory training.

Thus there is liveliness in the spontaneity of the IMPROVISER.

Mirror Image relating to the Myth Narcissus

The teacher needs to watch the growth and development of the theme. Is the class succeeding in creating the environment of woodland, forest, idyllic glade?

Re-create the appearance, nature, actions and expression of the young god-like Narcissus.

Margaret: "I tried to force the character—I should have just let the situation take over—I suppose I was not completely involved. I didn't feel the situation, and I could not react sincerely."

Beatrix: "I was too idealistic. My own image was in the way and therefore I could not become Narcissus who fell in love with his own beauty. I should have used more serenely beautiful curved lines; my attention could have been more concentrated in a smaller area. I needed a better sense of timing as I reflected on my image and actions, which I imagined I could see in the water."

Julia: "She seemed puzzled; afraid. Her arms were lyrical with beautiful designs in the air. She needed to be more vital in her movements."

Maria: "Her imagination worked quickly and came alive. Her stylised movements were youthful and strong. She forgot herself and was swept along by the topic. She became the young god. She created the best atmosphere in her facial expression, smile and feeling in her impressions of the state of falling in love. She created a response between herself and the imaginary reflection."

Fiona: "This topic is outside my experience. I lost touch with the real and imaginary feelings."

My Comments to the Class

What is the use of limiting the meaning of the improvisation? If the dance is to have meaning, it should surely be expressive of the human experience?

Narcissus could be translated into a figure in our own time. A vain girl, or youth, carried away by their own beauty—full of conceit, pompous and foolish; ending in grief: pathetic, helpless.

Dance movements for the studied stylised curved poses and balances of this mythical creature, could be sustained and connected to each other. Light flutterings of hands and feet and quick movements of head, expressive of the weird stillness and sounds of the forest.

Restraint, harmony and unity, lyrical movement; quick and sudden changes of direction; small jumps; twistings and hoppings, a piquant style as the god flirts capriciously with his own image.

Mirror Image: **Birthday of the Infanta**—Based on the fairy story by Oscar Wilde.

Your need of knowledge of yourself, your style, your capacity to release the imagination.
Characteristics:
Infanta: spoilt, proud, arrogant, Spanish, haughty, cruel, domination, defiance, royal, rejection.
Dwarf: ugly, deformed, awkward, suffering, pity, twisted, introverted, pleading.

Dialogue between dance students and me.

"The slow strong movements of Meggan as the Infanta expressed pride, arrogance, cruelty. Her strong dramatic feeling seemed to motivate her imperial gestures."

"Pathetic-distorted: Julie, as the dwarf reacted with deep feeling when she confronted her image in the mirror. She became misshapen, as her body bent forwards, making distorted and twisted shapes.

"The slow peacock-like dance movements by Beatrix expressed much of the power and cruelty in the young Infanta's nature as she taunted and mocked the dwarf who declared his love for her. She set her theme of movement and then made the theme grow, changing the pace as she developed the meaning and emotion of the character. A feeling of resistance in her oppositional movements gave her an expression of power."

The sad plight of the dwarf was depicted by feverish, shrinking gestures and movements. The student accentuated frustration and hopelessness by alternating lines of tension, and the weaker lines of parallel. The design of improvisation finished with Meggan executing slow falls to the floor, expressive of the figure of the dwarf, who died of a broken heart.

One needs to develop a feeling for the improvisational experience—a facility for individualised movement—a release of expression—and an understanding of the creative act through which one can satisfactorily develop concepts.

*　　　*　　　*

An Imaginary Being

Let us create an imaginary being.[63] Visualise yourself as a strange creature—mysterious, elusive, vague but aware, with a definite shape. You may be an animal, bird, fish, vegetable or reptile. Explore the upside down world of the poltergeist—demons, elves.

Your shape will change and your movement must show your appearance—smooth, spiny, scaly, segmented, thick, transparent or fleshy. You may develop wings or grow tentacles. Your legs may be joined or you might carry your shell on your back. You might float, swim or shuffle in your strange world.

Experiment with the way you will move. You could take the weight of your body on your back or on other parts of your body. Your body shapes might become more and more complex. Your fantastic shape will have a deeper meaning. It will be a symbol of your inner state whether you reflect fear or timidity, cruelty or frustration.

Some imaginary shapes can reflect your idea of beauty—arms and hands of filigree or circular movements as in the eyes of the peacock. Tenderness and delicacy of feeling are essential in the representation into dance of the continuous fragile waving of the anemone.

63 Inspired by the book of Imaginary Beings by J. L. Borges. Music by Robert Parris, also based on the Imaginary Beings by Louis Borges.

Conceive your image through your imagination. Nurture the creative feelings of childhood to adulthood. In mirror reflection there is another reference to man's reactions to his reflection. J. L. Borges adds another dimension to Mirror Reflection in his two stories: "The Double" and "Fauna of Mirrors". In "The Double", he reveals to us the strange implications of man's exact counterpart. "Fauna of Mirrors" illustrates for us the Chinese belief in the elusive magical arts of mirrors.

In the writings of Poe and Wilde, man's reaction is fearful, horrified and mystified by the discovery of his other self. Relate your reaction to the characteristics of human nature.

Dance composition based on the myth—Apollo and Hiacinthus
(Refer to page 126)
Photography: E. Waite

12   Immediacy

...of the present ... the city.

Find something that is real *or* imaginary and represent it through the dance.

Try to capture the essence of the original and then add your own statement giving it a new twist, finding the hidden potential in the shape, the atmosphere, or the feeling of the substance.

Make your students aware of different sources of inspiration. Talk, show, read to them—poetry, painting, music, art and dance, history, colour, critical essays—all the things pertaining to the Arts—become alive to Art and Culture. The adventurous spirit—the real, the imaginary, the aesthetic—of taste and imagination.

Build a work from the *Immediacy of the Present*—anything that attracts your curiosity, or that you notice as you come through the city.

We read *South Side* by Alexander Franklin. It tells us of an area around London Bridge.

> Sights, Sirens, Smells, Shouts. Of Labour, Strength, Sweat. Of Ships, Docks, Warehouses.

> The Dynamic movements of Dockhands, Labourers, Drivers.

We look at reproductions of paintings by Franz Kline (American painter).

The opposing physical forces holding bridges and buildings in balance, the thrusts and angles of steel girders, kindled in us the thoughts of the tension and conflict in Life.

WHAT WE SEE

> People rushing about.

> The fog clouding the city—like sleep.

> Mechanisation—agitated shapes.

> Symbols of man's restlessness and striving.

> Patches of green.

Fruit barrows, fruit shops, markets, gossip.

Laughter.

Young lovers.

People waiting—

—you don't know where they come from or where they are going—
They just hover.

Old Age—they are absorbed, dreaming; they are so close to death.

Loneliness, softness, melancholy, gaiety, harshness, vulgarity.

Poor and rich.

Handsome men, ladies of fashion.

Children playing.

Balancing like an acrobat on scaffolding.

Escalation.

The swallowing up of people as they rush into subways.

A red scarf next to a yellow umbrella.

Purple, blue and gold of a stained glass window.

Find a place for them in your improvisations. Let your language of expression
(movement) evolve with each new situation.

Build in the space.

Let us see (on many levels) your planal formations; vertical, horizontal and
the continuity of the linear; the smooth and angular shapes; swirling forms;

> changing of flexed arms and legs;

> The gentle curves of fluid movement;

> Vivacious hops and skips;

> Slow and stately walks—

>> dignity, seriousness.

> Quick and slow easy looseness,

>> —swinging of jazz;

Power and force of hard and precise oppositions.

Hollowed out, closed, narrow body—dejection

Dance rhythms displaying action.

Precise small movements, quaint and delicate.

Leaps and jumps carrying the body into space with a driving force.

The body poised—a dance gesture.

Quick change of direction

slowing down, speeding up.

The total action is an accumulation of a series of great and small movements (not repeated) which have evolved from the first movement, with an emotional response, and a feeling of expression giving meaning to the work.

Keep working together as much as possible, for as long as possible, to develop an appreciation, understanding, and ANTICIPATION of what each one wants to say.

*   *   *

...of the Past ... the Myth

Of all subjects chosen for the dance, the myth seemed to hold for us a certain fascination. From time to time some of my students discussed the possibility of creating a work involving the exploits of gods and heroes—perhaps of presenting an age-old traditional rite. Whether our pre-occupation came from a hidden desire to discover the roots of our origin, or the secret of the universe, I cannot tell. But we wanted to examine works concerned with a spiritual meaning, "with the powers of nature, the origin of created things".[64]

The myth based on Hades and the Underworld, was created by a class of year ten students (average age 15 years). This class wanted something of a dramatic nature to work on. They were not inclined towards dance technique for its own sake, and they wanted to involve themselves with a theme which was interesting in characterisation and dramatic motivation.

Hades then was the very thing! It evolved from purely improvisational exercises and the patterns and groupings arose out of the context. The improvisational angle diminished after some weeks of working, and the overall body shape, changes and directions of individuals and groups were firmly etched in the memory; the spontaneity of expression and the excitement of innovation began to disappear to be replaced by a unity borne of composition.

The following description is in the form of introductory notes, whereby you can follow our realisation and interpretation of this traditional story. The simplicity yet effectiveness and range of the movement sequences supported the dramatic idea of the legendary piece.

The idea then was to create a wide landscape—to fill the space with clusters of expressive figures significant of the actions of the drama. These were the River Styx, Hades, Charon the ferryman, Cerebus the watchdog, the shadows, the burdens and the souls of the dead.

64 *Mythology of all Races*, John C. Ferguson; Marshall Jones & Co., Boston.

1. The predominant moveing shape for the River Styx was a broken curve design—two lines of figures lying down, spaced out on the floor. They tossed and swirled their bodies, winding and unwinding, creating an effort of restlessness and unquiet. A perpetual change of movement—an ebb and flow of semi-circular movement—of legs, arms, back and head—within this serpentine shape.

2. The Hades figure was rather in the nature of a heroic majestic character. The movement in this theme was strong, percussive, strong-opposition, elongated extensions of legs, sudden arrests of movement with the body held poised in a balance, or air-borne in leap. The impressiveness was further heightened by the use of a length of red and black material which was flung boldly into the air like a flag or mysteriously coiled snake-like around the body of the Hades figure. This figure communicated the rest of the dramatic content to the groups by summoning them to action by high, wide, open expansive arm gestures. Large monumental body shapes, deep lunges, runs and leaps and widespread arm and leg action; this central figure united the action of the scene. Veronique crystallised all this in the simple grandeur of her role.

3. Once the shape of the river and the Hades figure had been determined, the focal point in this design was selected. Charon, the ferryman began to develop. The movement was a series of long, slow, continuous pulling and stroking arm movements. The slant of the body of Charon, leaning backwards as it were into the past, to draw the dead soul figures into the river, then the tilting forwards as if to thrust them toward their future fate. Tautness and sparseness.

4. From an opening in the river design, a group of figures emerged—the dead souls. These legendary characters used twisted and contorted body shapes; sudden back falls to the floor; walking on the knees with arms outstretched in supplication. They expressed themselves in a procession of torment and compassion; of hopelessness and despair; of emotional content through the medium of the human body in movement.

5. At another point in the overall floor pattern, one of the students crouched as Cerebus the dog. Sharp, geometric angles, the figure squatted low to the floor. When the legs were lifted, they were bent and the feet flexed. At all times the body was in a crouching position, arms and hand were jabbing and angular. Macabre and grotesque.

6. At the perimeter of the space, the groups of students gathered. These were the shadows and the burdens.[65] The shadows travelled for a time on the floor, creeping forward with long stretches of the body

---

65 These characters are not in the original text of the myth. We created them to give a feeling of greyness and doom to the piece.

and legs. They heightened the mood of their character by covering themselves with long pieces of grey filmy material. The material was painted with splashes of black and silver and the effect was luminous and moon-like. They crossed the space like a freize. Moving in unison, they glided along on their toes. As they sped along, they enfolded themselves in their silvery shrouds, wraith-like, with a delicate textured grace.

I was reminded of the line from the poem of Emily Dickinson:
"Presentiment is that long shadow on the lawn."

The burdens moved with a feeling of heaviness and weight. They arranged their group in levels, yet all were connected. They intertwined their arms and their steps were close to the ground. Long slow lunges and dragging steps with their bodies curved inwards, the group produced an expression of sorrow and oppression. To break the slow monotonous movement an arm would shoot upwards, a hand would open suddenly, a head would be thrown back. They travelled across the floor entwined together in a whirling mass. When they reached the end of the river design they moved into a new composition of dramatic contrast.

The movement changed to become symmetrical, reposeful, serene. The outstretched arms, lifted chest and outward glance expressed tenderness and peace. They had entered the Elysian fields. They presented an expression of harmony and calmness. All design was rounded and even. All steps light. All twisting and weaving about each other was gentle and ethereal and lyrical.

This may give you an indication of the way in which we tackled the themes within this particular legend.
The groups worked on their movement sequences consistently until they were satisfied that they were convincing and that we had met the requirements of the idea. Then the groups changed and there was a new shifting of characterisation. Everyone was given a chance to develop new material, infusing the same topic with a new interpretation.

13   Dance Poems

"I Sing the Body Electric"[66]

An exploration into the Possibilities of Movement of the Body and Parts of the Body.

Somewhere in our experience of building the dynamic principles of creativity, I tried to make a connection between pure movement experimentation in the craft of the dance, and a purpose or an idea which could be communicated. It is necessary to guide the student to see their technique as an outgrowth of a personal need for expression. The subject matter can be conceived within an area of experience. Try to make the movements evolutionary, that is, growing out of one into another—an emergence, a flow of movement—give it little twists that are unpredictable. Arrange the time and space sequences in whatever order you choose.

The group of students to whom I introduced "I Sing the Body Electric" had all completed about 3, 4 and 5 years dance; technical and creative. The standard of work was reasonably high and they understood the creative process.

They were ready for another idea that would stimulate movement—I chose Walt Whitman because in this particular poem he glorifies movement. He sings of the body, poetry and the dance, as singular art forms which can develop independently, yet interact at a specific point.

Try to move simply, not only as a physical experience, but feel the movement in terms of a spiritual projection of your feeling—deal with it in terms of your own experience—your own insights.

In the poem, Walt Whitman idealises the body, youth, health, vigour and aliveness. There is vigour in your temperament and your efforts are praiseworthy. The language is praiseworthy and bursting with life, but with a reverence for life. He rejoices in the body and its parts. There is an exultation in being alive. We should be proud of the fact that we are that marvellous human being.

His song is of the perfect female and the perfect male. It is linked with movement, with admiration and concern.

Excerpts from the text of the poem:[67]

66 "I Sing the Body Electric", from the Children of Adam; Leaves of Grass by Walt Whitman.

67 Extracts from the text of the poem "I Sing the Body Electric".

Flexed Jump
Photograph : Anthony Horth

Leap

Photograph: Anthony Horth
Stretch both legs in the
space; both arms open; (palms out)
and simultaneously arch the body

"The man's body is sacred,

and the woman's body is sacred,

. . .

Each has his or her place in the procession.

. . .

Within runs blood,

the same old blood! The same red-running blood!

There swells and jets a heart, there all

passions, desires, reachings, aspirations,

. . .

This is the female form,

The female contains all qualities and tempers them,

She is in her place and moves with perfect balance."

Whitman sings and delights in the parts of the body, for example:

"Head, neck, hair, eyes, mouth, tongue, teeth,
nose, cheeks, throat, back of the neck, upper
arms, armpit, lower arm, wrist, wrist-joint,

hand, palms, knuckles, forefinger, breast-bone,

hips, hip-socket, hip-strength inward and outward,

ribs, strong set of thighs, leg-fibres, knee,

upper-leg, ankles, instep, foot, toe-joints,

the heel: All attitudes, all the shapeliness

all the belongings of my or your body, or of any

one's body, male or female . . .

the brain, womanhood, the voice, articulations,

whispering shouting aloud . . .

the beauty of the waist. The exquisite

realization of health.

O I say, these are not the parts and poems of

the body only,
but of the soul,

O I say now 'these are the soul'!"

In terms of the dance there is so much movement in this declaration of the body and its parts.

Contraction
Photograph: Douglas Thompson
Contract pelvis; at same time
one leg is raised and bent and
arms curve to follow
semicircular line of the body
in contraction

I read parts of the poem to the class. We agreed that there was much scope for total body movement and with particular parts of the body. There should be some interesting use of dynamics, as parts of the body will be best expressed by certain dynamic movements, for example, heels will be staccato, or forceful; knees, sharp action; fists short and sharp.

I began to move among the class which was spread out on the floor. Some were standing or kneeling, others lying—all were facing in different directions. At first I wanted them to work individually and then join in movement with their nearest partner—then build up into clusters of 3 and 4's. They could break off and form their movement as an individual again.

I began to see movement—The beginning of life—Exploratory—Reaching out.

"Ankles and wrists rotating, feet flexing in all directions—elbows jabbing sharp and pointed, and knees punching, one or more body parts becoming co-ordinated.

"Push harder, stronger; become a shape. Most turned into engines, machines which suited these parts of the body. Hard, precision-like movement of wrists, ankles, elbows, knees and vertical movement of the straight and bent leg. Precision piston-like."

Then into the embracing and enfolding of the body and the arms, wide legs curved forward and backward in supple bends.
Running and arching the chest and extending the arms. Head free, lifted upwards.

> "Separate your fingers—rotate separately your fingers inward and out-ward—like the hands of the Spanish dancer—fan-like. Arch your back, contract your upper body, twist; Slow, or quick fall to the ground."

The wide, open, expansive movements—everything radiates outward. Legs circle from front through side to back; successive arches of the body.

Spinning and turning. The closing and opening of the arms, chest and upper body.

Body tilts—leg extensions—balance—one leg takes the weight, the body is poised precariously in the space.

"Now leave the floor, leap, jump into the space—use your arms in a way in which you have never combined them before. Wide, high, legs stretched, legs bent, body stretched or body curved in an arc. Move into the space upwards and downwards. Bend the body deeply in all directions; release the back; rotate the hips; flex the foot."

"Fill the spatial dimension with the dynamics of movement. Your body is your individual instrument in your artistic expression."

During the successive lessons, I isolate some of the parts so that we work more deeply; more variations of movement, more drama, more lyricism:

> "The expression of the face,
>
> The flex of the knees, carriage of the neck,
>
> The female soothing a child,

The bent head, the curved neck.

Leaping, reclining . . .

Toes."

If a head was lifted, you felt that the eyes, face, neck, backbone were all involved. The head could make a proud symbol.

"Use the legs to thrust the body forward into space or lower it to the ground —turn the head in one direction and twist the body in another." A mobile neck—wide, open, extensions; we create an outward going, liberty loving expression. The positive movement is all affirmation of joy and energy. To walk, to run, to fall, to leap, to intertwine, to separate, to advance and retreat, to balance, to pause."

"Consciously feel the movement. Do not accept the first action that you think of—work harder to find a better movement and improve the design— symmetry (all equal) asymmetry (one part of the body in an unequal design to the other parts), curves, twist and distortion."

"You are all part of this vast group moving on the floor, relate and associate then in turn become part of something else. Create a new focal point, a new cluster of movements, a new design, a new sequence. Gesture! Spontaneity! Dynamics!"

"To give your work eloquence and power, it must spring from the breath and grow organically, that is from inside. It springs from the centre of your body."

"You will need to shape the body[68] and deepen the movement. Look to the articulation of the fingers, the curve of the back, renew the tensions in the body; fall; slide; twist; contract; circle; roll."

"Parallelism in standing, and in moving, and in the air, legs bent or stretched, taut, articulate."

"Each part of the body has its own special qualities and you have to discover a way to make it responsive.."

The conception of one's own body design and the inspiration of the words from the poem will project upon the imagination. What we need to do is to continually deepen the awareness of movement and eliminate the unessential, the movement that says nothing.

"Do not feel compelled to fill the space with empty movements or gestures but rather to think again of this quotation."

"And what of that infinite and beautiful thing dwelling in space, called movement?"[69]

Dance Poem—"Let no Light be Shed on Me" *(by Maria, year ten, age sixteen years)*

> "In every life there is a stronger need—
> To have someone,
> Not having, I wrap myself in sorrow.

68 Martha Graham.

69 Edward Gordon Craig.

Oh life so lonely
Let no light be shed on me.
I shall ignore it,
I know there is no such thing—
'Tis but an illusion.
But stop—
Then why not having it am I so wretched?
I must find it!
With first step uncertain
Where to look?
Shall I wander aimlessly?
No . . . I see a light,
I run to capture it—

   This is love!
So soft it gently flutters above my head.
My fingers reach
Too high
I jump
Caught!
And it is mine.
Round and round and round—
What is this dizziness?
I feel no pain,
I'm out of darkness, out of distress.
'Tis magic, a realm of bliss
My heart leaps for joy
Oh happy hour!
I have found it, I have found it
A tidal wave surges up inside me
Lost in a world of bliss, happiness, fulfilment—
I feel rest, peace of mind and a joy that cannot be related
Love—a dream?
Then let me not awaken
Nor take me out of this fantasy
For 'tis a cloud I fly through
An ecstasy, a realm of magic.

   Collapsed—gone.
Fascination disrupted
Rudely brought back to reality.
Oh how cold the world is
How unwanted!

Where is love? Oh love
But Heaven's affliction whose arrows pierce the heart—
Oh sad pain
Why do you smile?

But happy grief
I had—I did have
But I have no more.
Oh heavy burden of my heart
Oh wretched pain within me
I cry
Let no light be shed on me."

Maria:
"After my poem was read we found that it had expression and feeling. Each girl thought deeply on the true essence of this feeling—love."

We discussed the emergence of the different personalities.

It wasn't difficult to decide which girl should become what aspect of love.

Julie's frail air, straight line, and melancholy colouring, suggested the first reaction—the realisation—the want, Julie expresses puzzlement and bewilderment quite effectively, thus she seemed the right choice for the part—her movements had to be broken in their rhythm.

Lola, having lyrical vitality and strong technique, seemed suitable for the climax—the bliss, the joy, happiness, and fulfilment.

The last section of the poem called for someone dramatic who could express frustration, turmoil and anguish. Beatrix's dark hair, dramatic and serious air, and ability, made her an appropriate choice.

During many months the poem was read, the imagery discussed, and the meaning in each section was brought out.

Julie started to improvise as the poem was read, trying to completely involve herself in the meaning of the words and the emotion of her part. Movements which particularly appealed to Meg, Beatrix and me were thought about and carried out. Each dancer was to put emotions and feelings into actions and movements.

Julie's part was developed by improvising and re-improvising. Alterations were made and important points brought out.

If Meg and I didn't agree with any movement suggested, we would argue about why we thought it was inappropriate and suggest another more suitable movement, again considering the meaning and the dance form.
Every girl helped form Lola's part.

Beatrix's part was both improvised and choreographed. We tried to bring out the theme of "Don't dance it, feel it". Her part was greatly pondered over and different lines were improvised.

135

In each dance piece, the three different aspects of love were expressed. The girls tried to invent movements rather than use steps that they had learned in their classes—the first aspect, full of fragmented gracefulness, especially in the arms, captured uncertainty. In the second part big, expressive, curved—reaching out, lyrical movements captured the joy. Both symmetry and asymmetry were used in the severe, noble movements in the third part.

"Beatrix danced it with feeling and it conveyed a deep, tragic sense", said Maria.

The Forest   *(Fort Street Dance Group)*
Photograph: Robert Walker
(Painting by Kerri Mahony)

14   SEARCHING OUT THE QUESTION OF DANCE

"The Art of dancing stands at the source of all the arts that express themselves first in the human person."[70]

70 The Dance of Life, by Havelock Ellis.

There were always opinions to be expressed on the question of dance, and wherever there happened to be a discussion in progress I would usually join in—sometimes merely to listen, at other times to fling myself into the mound of words that were tumbling out about Dance—feeling and sensitivity, technique, movement, creativity.

In the ensuing discussion are some comments and viewpoints by members of Fort Street Dance Group and a few senior dance students. I heard different attitudes by these young people, who are, now that their labour and efforts have made the modern or contemporary dance a reality in their lives, prepared to wrestle with the meaning of Dance, as part of our culture and its significance in education.

Discussion:

Meg: I think everyone should be given the chance to dance and to create. It is like a journey.
You discover more and more about yourself and others. You begin to realise that your body can move outside the same old boring movements. Your hand, for instance, does NOT move merely to hold objects or perform routine tasks—I can move with a new shapeliness.

Adrienne: The dance for me has a physical, emotional and spiritual life.

Elizabeth: I once read somewhere that "dance is the unalloyed expression of the soul". For me, that is, in *my* dancing, I must find a kind of purity of expression—a concentrated purity about something I feel, and which I can dance with meaning—with significance.

Vera: I think of dance as a work of art by the body in movement. To use the movements of the modern dance in ways which express an idea based on human values. Dance helps me to become aware of the many individual characteristics of the external life around me and of my own inner life. I have become more aware of how the individual is caught up and reacts to the human situation—I am interested in interpreting these feelings of life; the result of life on people; the fears of a child; the shock of intense cold; restriction and denial; poverty; an icy wind.

Debbie: Can the modern dance help people to become more aware of the futility of wars and start them thinking more about the human suffering in the world?

Meg: The good and evil in Man and his relationship with others and the meaning of events and actions, can be shown in the dramatic content.

Caroline: But surely we can see and hear and read about human experiences through other ways besides the dance?

Meg: The thoughts and feelings of an onlooker may be touched more deeply perhaps and stirred by a dance experience.

Cherie:	How?
Meg:	Because they can see and feel and live the situation which is being presented to them.
Cherie:	There would have to be a very sympathetic response between the one watching and the one who was dancing.
Adrienne:	There would have to be communication.
Meg:	Yes, and if there was that connection between the two, then the one who was watching could be moved to think about the content and value of the work.
Elizabeth:	And perhaps be jolted out of their complacency!
Meg:	If there is no communication, then the onlooker's interest will wander and there won't be much thought.
Cherie:	Dance can be fun and humorous, cheerful and serene—it is not only showing us problems and suffering.
Vera:	And the onlooker should be as well informed as the dancer.
Caroline:	That presents a challenge of being dance educated—ready to understand a subject and its moods and emotions.
Debbie:	But not everyone will react in the same way and their opinions will be different.
Caroline:	Yes, but as long as they *do* react.
Debbie:	Then the dancer needs to be able to project the emotions, feelings and moods of the work, with expression and belief.

On technique:

Janet:	What has been the response from the students to the classes in modern dance technique? Do they recognise the fact that if they want freedom to move, and yet control over their movement they need to learn the disciplines of technique?
C.H. (author)	Some bodies respond sooner and more easily to the dance training and this usually depends on the way the student approaches the training and on the physical build. Flexibility, balance, strength, control, co-ordination are only developed slowly and the actual physical work is difficult and painstaking—I try to give the classes an understanding of the need to overcome their fears of expressing themselves through movement—of building up the courage to break through the barriers of physical incompetence—to learn how their own bodies move, and to find a way of moving in which they can function as an expressive human being. They can then explore the creative aspect of the dance in their own way, with an instrument more sensitive to movement responses, and a mind open to the excitement of inventions.

I think that it is within the grasp of all dance students to achieve a good basic background of dance movement, while preserving in their minds that the approach to dance, through technique, will lead to the discovery and expressiveness of movement.

Janet: In other words, technique should not become meaningless and automatic.

C.H.: Technique is a means to an end. One has to put feeling and sensitive insight into a dance role. You need to dance with passion and conviction in order to move people.

Janet: In your teachings do you emphasise the theories and vocabulary of any special school of modern dance?

C.H.: Yes, it is based upon that of dance artists, Gertrud Bodenwieser, Martha Graham, Doris Humphrey and others. Throughout the years of involvement with dance I have had to constantly evaluate the body of dance knowledge that I have absörbed. One had to learn to develop. I have worked on, changed and reshaped ideas and material to suit the realities of a particular situation. One becomes aware of the different goals of dance in education and of the ways used to meet their creative and technical development. So I have had to constantly plan, analyse and experiment with different age groups —introducing new directions in movement with emphasis on new ideas, range and quality. Some of our more serious minded individuals have tried to find their own style, and project their own expressive personality.

Caroline: To do this, it seems to me we need to master the use of our bodies, and the technique should not look strained.

Vera: I enjoy disciplining my body so that it moves well for me.

Elizabeth: I like to make a beautiful line.

Adrienne: I like to understand a movement. It must feel right for my body and I need to be sure in what I am doing.

Debbie: Adrienne strives for perfection.

Caroline: Technique gives you the means of building up a dance vocabulary to a high degree—then you can begin to work on the quality of a movement.

Elizabeth: To me technique is only secondary and it is the development of your own personal expression and style that matters.

Cherie: Without feeling, dance is boring.

Caroline: Without the tensions and opposition and dissimilarities the dance is also dull. We don't need so much harmony in movement.

Vera: Too obvious, more contrast as in life.

Meg: More life in our movements.

Elizabeth: You should never become too dependent on technique, or let it get in the way of original, individual and spontaneous movement. I would like to see a new dance movement born—a range and style that was new and your own.

Adrienne: We are not all Isadoras, Elizabeth!

Elizabeth: I love to look at some of the younger children in your classes, Miss Hinkley, who have only been dancing for one or two years. What a joy they find in making up and, although they haven't learnt much technique, they dance with imagination and an unspoilt expressiveness.

Adrienne: Some of them look clumsy to me—and awkward.

Elizabeth: But they are individuals just the same, who are moving to express their own ideas—and moving freely out of the restrictions of a routine.

Caroline: But don't you think, Elizabeth, that once they have learnt how to move, they do it so much better.

Elizabeth: Many of them show the love for dance so much in the free expressive way in which they move.

Debbie: They move with a sense of fun and enjoyment and bounciness.

Vera: And enthusiasm—sometimes they just will not stop dancing—they seem possessed.

Adrienne: But we also leaped and stretched and ran and practised at the barre —we were always dancing. We improvised and we worked at our favourite movements. Then we began to realise that there was something deeper, and our ties with dance became stronger—we found that we needed to pay more attention to technique and we began to want to learn more and work more thoroughly, so that we would reach a higher level of dance.

Vera: For six years now we have been dancing; learning technique; exploring creative themes; improvising; some of us have had confidence to compose; we have experienced the demands of dance as an art form, rehearsals and performance. Dance has become an indispensable part of our lives.

Elizabeth: Yes; an inner necessity.

* * *

Horizons:

Helen: What of the expectations for those of us who want to progress at a faster rate?

Janet:	Dance Club; a time to meet together to dance more and become involved in the complexities of dance.
Elizabeth:	A time of concentration to try out our own ideas—a time to discuss our creative projects—
Vera:	An occasion to experiment with new ways of connecting movements; turns linked with jumps; experimenting with the fall; the possibilities of change in movement in space and time.
Elizabeth:	Taking part in the delight of the dance.
Caroline:	Contact with the other dance students in the school—an exchange of ideas.
Debbie:	The surge of movement.
Adrienne:	A time to create—to work on the problems and questions that arise when you begin to develop your idea.
Helen:	Sometimes even the mistakes are better than your original idea—
Janet:	The satisfaction you feel when you have developed your dance idea exclusively on your own.
Cheryl:	So many of the girls in the school ask: "Where can we join Dance Club?" "How good do you have to be?"
Debbie:	There are no special requirements—just as long as they enjoy what they are doing and are willing to try new ideas.
Meg:	I like teaching the younger ones and introducing them to our work in the early morning classes before school. I introduce some elementary dance technique, and then we talk about lines, and shapes, and try to improve their own way of growing through dance with an improvisation.
C.H.:	I have been very fortunate to have had the loyalty, co-operation, and deep feeling towards the dance from the many members of my dance group. They have been patient and inspiring in their teaching assistance towards the students in the dance club, to any member of the school who has something to ask about the materials of dance.

*   *   *

Questions and Answers:

Helen:	Do you design your dance programme for the average school student or for those with special aptitudes and abilities?
C.H.:	The programme is designed for all the students irrespective of ability or previous dance background. It is a comprehensive study of dance Technique, Creativity and Dance Theory and Appreciation. The

presentation of the selection and arrangement of these materials of dance and the different modes of expression, depend upon the level and progression of the classes.

A vocabulary of training in the modern dance, makes for expression and variety of movement for communication by means of action, for artistic and creative purposes.

Integration of the physical, creative, and aesthetic aspects of the craft, should flow towards the creative use of movement, and provide the individual with the experience to know dance as an art form, and as a vital source of personality development.

The growth in the child, of concepts, insight, expression of feeling and experience, is consistent with the aims of education; and these aims are explored in the dance curriculum by each student being brought into direct contact with the theories and practices of the substance of dance.

Helen: You want to develop us as creative human beings?

C.H.: Yes, I try to enrich your personal development, encouraging an awareness of human values, such as—

Independence

Courage

Tenacity

Curiosity

Originality

As you learn to work creatively, I became more aware of your personality. Your need to discover the kind of human beings you really are, and something about your contemporaries—to look around you—at the world outside yourselves.

If you are encouraged to observe people and your surroundings, and your reactions and experiences are related directly to the dance, you become more alert and aware and better equipped to express your concepts and images of the world you live in.

It is essential for the teacher to encourage the involvement of the students in creative work—freedom to discover movement, independence to develop their creative potential, and the inspiration for the urgency and fulfilment of communication.

Helen: Do you always divide the Theory and Practice of Creativity into two broad categories—Design for Dance with Themes and Creative Materials and Composition?

143

C.H.: That's right. I introduce improvisation into the study of creativity because I believe it is a device for cultivating the creative process.

I start the students improvising as soon as possible—not merely to "let off steam" or to release inhibitions, but as a disciplined freedom —to discover new ways of moving and to let the body become aware of this new movement experience—I encourage the students to move further and further into an expressive labyrinth of their own, away from the directed dance technique; drawing their inspiration from the world we live in, and from within themselves, and drawing their motivation purely from the movement.

Helen: There are so many different approaches to idea, mood or emotion —I like the action involving a theme.

C.H.: I don't think it matters what the motivation is—the most important thing is to leave the beaten track, and search for a new way to express your point of view. You have to find the way of working that suits you.

* * *

On Creativity:

Janet: Are the girls adventurous in their creative approach?

C.H.: To a greater or lesser degree most of them show curiosity, originality, spontaneity, flexibility and initiative when they choose to work creatively.

I vary the realisation of creativeness according to the age levels of each class; their self-insight and understanding of each other, and readiness to engage in an experience of an aesthetic nature; the rapport between them and myself.

Everyone should be attuned to the ideas, feelings, emotions and associations necessary for the creative activities at that moment. The classes will bring their poems, music, drawings, paintings and other imaginative material that may add a further dimension to their creative accomplishments—thereby extending their dimension as a human being and as a member of society—a creatively educated individual.

In the evaluation of the creative effort there are questions—
"Did you give it an expressive form?"
"Could you discipline your creative energies?"
"Was your approach honest—did it have freshness and quality and no exhibitionism?"

Although you may have found a point of view from which to begin your creative experiment it must develop logically and have meaning of some kind.

144

"Could be done better—more quality needed—too mechanical —rather like an exercise."

"Jumbled, baffling."

"Nothing happened."

"Did your body respond—could you find movements expressive of the theme?

Sometimes the class agreed that unity was achieved, and I have seen a plastic quality as the body discovered ways of moving, that grew, one out of the other—a continuity—not always predictable but movement language that has its own expressive meaning, shape and communication.

When this is achieved someone would say—

"That was beautiful."

"Moving."

"Musical colour."

"Night wind."

"Wild grasses."

"Like a summer landscape."

So much depends on the teacher who is guiding the creative behaviour. A free and exploratory discussion in which themes are suggested and discussed—insight into the idea as the groups become more sensitive to the meaning. Is the idea suitable for the dance and can it be translated into movement? Independent thought is encouraged in these discussions, and while some of the students prefer to passively accept the reactions and opinions of others, the more creatively-involved individuals express themselves freely with varied significance. *There must not be too much verbalising about the content at the expense of dance action*—the most significant moment takes place in terms of movement, when the theme, or *that which the dance is about* is shaped into a creative form. Whether the theme is based on a story, an emotion or is abstract, the student has to think in terms of movement and choose content which is appropriate to the experience.

The teacher needs to recognise and respond to the creative efforts making sure that the subject matter can be handled by the classes. Each exploration by the student is expressive of the child's artistic understanding and the one who is guiding the work needs a certain detachment when appraising or criticising the form. Knowledge, wise judgment, experience, artistic integrity, creative insight and thought-provoking assessment, of the creative workings of the individual's or the group's approach help shape the values, attitudes understanding and output of expressive material by the class. The creative work is dictated by the quality of movement. One may need to guide the class in the technical and creative approaches and all the situations could be different.

The situation should be challenging enough to provoke the aesthetic interest of each individual and although the teacher can help stimulate their creative fervour to experiment, each one in the class is the originator and director in the creative endeavour, analysing and outlining their own development in terms of action.

*   *   *

On Composition:

Helen: Can the Improvisational approach, whether its subject matter is movement or creative themes be resolved into a compositional form? By that, I mean can the elements of the creative form be co-ordinated so that the creative work can be recalled and repeated?

Janet: When we worked through the Improvisational approach and wanted to develop the themes as compositions for the dance programme, we had to unite our creative thought with action, thinking a great deal more about the formal elements of composition. If it was a group work we had to give and take and listen to other contributions—we had to keep on working on it until it was satisfying to do.

Helen: As in our dance composition for "Within You, Without You",[71] we had to work out and set the floor design for six dance students and then create the design for six bodies in the space.

Janet: Some of the direction was implied by the movement.

Helen: And a lot of the dance movements came out of the meaning and emotion.

C.H.:   You also had to find a title, give it a beginning, middle and end and select and arrange the improvisational material into an integrated dance work.

    I remember that you worked a long time on applying dynamics to the movement. You had to work on certain spots so that more energy would be released—more forceful movement—towards the climax you had to find the kind of movements that would be sharp and fast and bring the work to an abrupt end.

Janet: The work would have been colourless without the element of Dynamics.

Helen: Drums and Bells was partly improvisational, partly compositional.

71 "Within You, Without You"—composed by dance students, Janet and Helen—music by the Beatles. The conception of the idea—the pull between steadfast conformists and the individual.

C.H.: We developed Drums and Bells with music by Chavez, from an improvisational theme, then the symmetry, balance and harmony were set into a compositional form. These were set for specific moments in the form and between times much of the dance movement was improvised. The balance was upset by an improvisational exploration where "contrast, inbalance, asymmetry and rhythmic speeds"[72] were skilfully integrated to give a feeling of tension—a unity between the known and the unknown.

This was a work full of complex relationships of interchanging floor patterns and contrasting dynamics; strong even and uneven, smooth and percussive movement. An abstract dance work with movement as its motivation, and the abstraction evoking a meaning —an emotion. It was an attempt to bring into focus a shadow that haunts our world today—of restless searching—of people rushing towards an abyss of no meaning.

Sally: In "Bells and Drums" the movements are hard and rather stereotyped. This depicts for me people surging through some dank, dungeon-like railway station; an accident in their pathway disturbs their regular regime; they stare bewildered, but minds completely occupied with destination, these callous beings depart hastily. Weaving through the shemozzle is an observer, brilliantly mechanised and placid, while time moves on to Chavez's jangly music.

Helen: "Haiku",[73] composed by a group of dance students, was developed in accordance with the principles of dance composition.

Janet: It was too literal at first in its interpretation. Too much movement. The word for word, movement for movement interpretation had to be scrapped.

Helen: Then they designed their dance form from a mood or image, or an association.

C.H.: They had to plan the space for each dance with smooth transitions between each verse. There was a lot of conscious working on the flow of movements—smooth and even, explosive, energetic and short; heavy and restrained. It seemed to capture the lyrical and dramatic expression inherent in the content of each verse.

Helen: Which experience do you think the students prefer—creating through an improvisational source or through the more formal process of composition or choreography?

C.H.: I think the young student needs as broad a range of creative experience as possible, if she is to develop her imagination and express her ideas. Not all studies lead to dances; some of them are developed into longer compositions and do, in fact, become dance works. By

72 Succession, opposition, unison. Doris Humphrey.

73 The dance work "Haiku" was based on the Japanese verse-form Haiku—one of the students wrote her own poems and the dance students converted them into a dance form.

presenting the student with the two sources (Improvisation and Composition) for development of their material in an original way, one acquaints them with the procedures for creative work—they discover in themselves resources that they were not aware of before.

Once they have been introduced by me to the different creative approaches and are secure in their understanding and knowledge about creative activity, they can choose any way that they prefer, to express themselves creatively. They can select their own approach to say something in dance. This is a chance for the experienced teacher, educated in dance, to apply a more specialised approach to the organisation of material for expressive purposes, through the formal approach, which is the study of dance composition or choreography; the arrangement and practice of movements arising from an inner need; combining the vocabulary of the modern dance (movement), with the essential elements of composition, (the means by which you are able to state your idea). These elements which have been agreed upon by dance educators and professional dancers here and abroad, are intended to assist the individual in achieving the form or structure, which is the framework of the dance.

This skill in working creatively is the whole purpose of the dance in education—to give a chance to those who have an idea and confidence and encouragement to others to try to compose, and never to discourage or stifle the creative urge. Strengthening the potential creative ability is, in particular, the responsibility of those who are concerned with the dance as a means of developing the individual; the importance of saving the creative ability, our most precious asset, is described by Arnold Toynbee[74] in his paper on the attitude to creativity in our "democratic" society—

"The Creator was withheld from the shark's teeth, the bird's wings, the elephant's trunk and the hound's or horse's racing feet. The creative power planted in a minority of mankind has to do duty for all the marvellous physical assets that are built into every specimen of man's non-human fellow creatures. If society fails to make the most of this one human asset, or if, worse still, it perversely sets itself to stifle it, man is throwing away his birthright of being the lord of creation and is condemning himself to be, instead, the least effective species on the face of the planet."

*   *   *

74 United States Stifles Creativity; Democracy and Conservatism Menace Creativity, by Arnold Toynbee—The New York University Alumni News, 1962.

"Making Up"
Photograph : Tony Baker

EPILOGUE

"Young dancers of the present and of the future, my last word is to you. Your way will be stony, your path will be hard, but to you will one day be the glory.

to have followed your convictions
undeterred by material hardships
or by the encasing wall of prejudice;

to have fought in the great revolution
of freeing the human mind;

to have lifted up a great art and placed it
on the pedestal of ethics
where it should stand;

to have shown that we dance
as we should endeavour to live:
in truth, simplicity and spirituality".[75]

---

75 Taken from the *New Dance* by Gertrud Bodenwieser. Reprinted with kind permission of Marie Cuckson M.A.—from the *New Dance* by Gertrud Bodenwieser, published by Rondo Studios, Sydney, for M. Cuckson. (Limited Edition No. 23.)

WORKS CHOREOGRAPHED BY CORALIE HINKLEY

for Fort Street Dance Group

Dance Films: Choros I (Dance); The Chairs
Bells and Drums (Chavez)

Choros II (Felix Werder) Mobile Sculpture by Bim Hilder

Dance for Five (Kodaly)

L'Isle Joyeuse (Debussy)

The Forest (Silence & Choreosonic Music by Alwin Nikolais)

Ritual for Dance, Play & Magic (Henry Cowell)

*   *   *

Coralie Hinkley chose Fort Street Dance Group, which now no longer exists, from the members of the Dance Club. This group aspired to acquaint themselves with the creative art—to more and more better dancing during some part of *every* day.

They were willing to respond to the goals of performance and to work for perfection in the emotional physical and intellectual framework of the contemporary dance.

They began to understand the truth of a theory of Picasso, that to achieve freedom in one's work one must be disciplined and that one must think deeply about one's work. They began to explore their own individual, interpretive qualities, extending and heightening their range of dance expression, noting that "Art is the most intense mood of Individualism that the world has known".[76]

76 *The Soul of Man under Socialism*—by Oscar Wilde.

CRITIQUES

"Coralie Hinkley sought soft, flowing movement for her choreography for L'Isle Joyeuse while in The Forest, her creatures were like disembodied, yet animate things that balanced and tottered or flailed; arms then torso then the whole body in tortured circlings of unemotional motion, as if instinct impelled and ordered all their distilled chaos."

(Beth Dean, The Sydney Morning Herald, September 22, 1970)

*   *   *

"Coralie Hinkley in 'Ritual for Dance, Play and Magic', managed to avoid the temptation to indulge her female emotions and in the process moved her large squad of girls about the stage with precision and imagination to considerable effect . . . a certain amount of cool objectivity does seem a necessary pre-requisite of a good choreographer. It is a complicated business."
(Brian Hoad, The Bulletin, May 29, 1971)

*   *   *

"The Arts in the Schools." Front cover and commentary on dance. "In spite of the general deficiencies outlined above, excellent dance programmes are being offered in some schools. These are the more remarkable because of their rarity at Fort Street G.H.S. Programmes in creative dance have for many years been an integral and cherished part of the Physical Education Programme."

1974

Student Compositions that were included in films or lecture-demonstrations or performances

The Net.

"I am alone with the beating of my heart" (Liu Chi).

Haiku.

Aerodybulide.

"Within you, without you".

Skratachapok.

Rochejac. (In video-tape film — CHOROS).

"Let No Light be Shed on Me". (In video-tape film — CHOROS).

"Apollo and Hiacinthus".—Student film.

Demonstrations and Performances

1963 *Onwards*

Day of Dance at Frensham; British Drama League Festival; Paddington Arts Festival; Northside Festival of the Arts; Dance Presentation, Sydney Teachers' College; Analysis of Technique and Composition, Sydney Teachers' College; Demonstration Lessons in Modern Dance Technique, development of thematic dance material for creativity; Improvisational Technique and Compositional Devices for Student Teachers in Art and Physical Education at Sydney Teachers' College and Alexander Mackie Teachers' College; Dance Works performed at The Captain Cook Bi-Centenary Celebrations; Ballet Australia Programmes—1970; The Australian Choreographic Competition—1971.

1969

The Chairs—Commonwealth Film Unit. Australian diary No. 133. 1971 Choros (I Dance); Video-tape film of choreography, creativity and dance technique, made by the faculty of education, Physical Education Department, Sydney University. Special Award for cultural and educational merit in Benson and Hedges Award for closed circuit television.

1972

Inside Education (Front Cover) and interview, Department of Education publication.

1974

The Arts in the Schools.

CREATIVE DANCE RECORDS

Activity Records Inc.,
Freeport, New York, U.S.A.

B.B.C. Movement, Mime and Music Series, RESR5, RESR13, 12″ L.P.
(2 records).

Classroom Materials,
93 Myrtle Drive,
Great Neck, New York, 11021, U.S.A.

Freda Miller Records for Dance,
Albums 1–5,
131 Bayview Avenue,
Northport, New York, 11768, U.S.A.

His Masters Voice, Listen, Move and Dance, OXLP 7533

Hoctor Educational Records for Dance,
Waldwick, New Jersey, 07463, U.S.A.

Kay Ortmans Productions,
2005 Alba Road,
Ben Lomond, California 95005, U.S.A.

Kiwi Records, Music for Creative Dance, EA-134, 135, 136 (3 records).

Kiwi Records, Music and Movement, EA-131, 132, 133 (3 records).

Music for Creative Movement,
J. Exiner, W.G. Record Processing Co.,
W.G. 35/5/5608,
Melbourne, Australia.

Sarah Malament,
3215 Netherland Avenue,
New York, 10463, U.S.A.

W. & G., There's Movement in Music, W.G. 25/5/5378. Devised by Heather
Gell. (W.G. Record Processing Co., Melbourne, Australia).

Appreciation to Fort Street Dance Group and to other dance students who
appear in this book.
Elizabeth Hunt
Sondra Kalnins
Vera Bulovan
Janet Brown
Margaret Trotter
Helen Fong
Adrienne Leal
Caroline Lung
Debbie Mitchell
Brenda Ware
Lola Ralec
Sally Phillips
Jeannie Highet
Susan Voss
Joanne Strauss
Janet Calver
Frances Stuve
Toni Selden
Veronique Helmreich-Marsilien
Linda Bell
Joanne Byrnes
Elaine Fong
Barbara Wethered
Kara Mitchell
Vivian Petak
George Katsilis
Rollo and Sasha (St Joseph's Primary School, Newtown), from Creative Dance
Lesson by Gloria Paduano for Coralie Hinkley, (Lecturer in Dance, Good
Samaritan Teachers College, Sydney).

BIBLIOGRAPHY

The Art of Making Dances, Doris Humphrey, B. Pollack (ed.), Rinehart & Company Inc.
Art and Culture, Clement Greenberg, Beacon Press.
The Art and Science of Creativity, George Kneller, Holt, Rinehart, and Winston.
Art and Education in Contemporary Culture, Irving Kaufman, Macmillan, New York.
Alexander Calder, The Museum of Modern Art, New York.
At The Vanishing Point, Marcia B. Siegel, Saturday Review Press, N.Y.
A Book of Curves, E. H. Lockwood, Cambridge University Press.
The Borzoi Book of Modern Dance, A. Knopf, New York.
Creativity and its Educational Implications, John Wiley and Sons Inc., U.S.A.
The Creative Process, Brewster Ghiselin, Mentor Books.
Creative Dance in the Primary School, Joan Russell, Macdonald and Evans, London.
Creative Power, Hughes Mearnes, Dover Publications N.Y.
Creative Person and Creative Process, Frank Barron, Holt and Rinehart.
Changes: Notes on Choreography, Merce Cunningham, Something Else Press.
Creative Rhythmic Movement for Children, Gladys Andrews, Prentice Hall, U.S.A.
Creativity, P. E. Vernon, Penguin.
Creative Dance, Janelle Cust, Physical Ed. Pub. Co-Op., Sydney.
Creative Rhythmic Movement: Boys and Girls Dance, Gladys Andrews, Prentice Hall.
Creative Intuition in Art and Poetry, Jacques Maritain, Meridian Books, New York.
Dance and Dance Drama in Education, V. Bruce, Pergamon Press.
Dance We Must, Ted Shawn, Lord Dennis Dobson.
Dance a Creative Art Experience, Margaret N. H'Doubler, University of Wisconsin Press.
The Dance of Shiva, Ananda K. Coomaraswamy.
The Dance in Art, Elli Lohse-Claus, Abbey Library, London.
The Dance of Life, Havelock Ellis, Grosset.
Dance an Art in the Academie, Teachers College Press.
Dance Composition and Production, Elizabeth Hayes, The Ronald Press Co.
Essays in Aesthetics, Jean-Paul Sartre, Peter Owen.
Expressive Movement and the Arts, Ruth St. Denis, Lepus Books, London.
Expressions in Movement: A Philosophical Inquiry, David Best, Lepus Books, London.
Experimental Dance, John Percival, Studio Vista.
Effort, Rudolph Laban, Macdonald and Evans.
Experimental Music, Lejaren A. Hiller, Leonard M. Isaacson, McGraw Hill.
Eurythmy and the Impulse of Dance, Rudolf Steiner.
Form, Space and Vision, Graham Collier, Prentice Hall.
Feeling and Form, Susanne K. Langer, Charles Scribner's Sons, New York.
Foundations of Modern Art, Ozenfant, Dover Publications.
History of Dance, Richard Kraus, Prentice Hall.
Haiku in English, Charles E. Tuttle Co.
Handbook for Modern Educational Dance, Valerie Preston, Macdonald and Evans.
Improvisation, John Hodgson and Ernest Richards, Methuen and Co. Ltd.
Journal of Aesthetic Education, Harvard University Press.
The Language of Dance, Mary Wigman, Macdonald and Evans.
Malraux, edited by R. W. B. Lewis, Yale University Press.
Modern Dance Forms, Louis Horst, Carroll and Russel, Impulse Publications.
Mastery of Movement; and *Modern Educational Dance*, Rudolf Laban.
My Life in Movement, Margaret Morris, Peter Owen.
Modern Dance Terminology, Paul Love, Karmin Dance Publishers.
The Modern Dance, John Martin, Karmin.
The Many Worlds of Dance, Walter Sorrell, Continental Publishing Co.
Martha Graham, Barbara Morgan, Duell, Sloan and Pearce.
Modern Dance, Jane Winnearls, Adam & Charles Black.

Materials of Dance, Barbara Mettler, Mettler Studios.
Modern Dance, Esther E. Pease, Wm. C. Brown Co.
Modern Dance, Gertrude Shurr, Rachael Dunaven Yocum, A.S. Barnes & Co.
The New Dance, Gertrud Bodenwieser, Rondo Studios.
Nine Articles for Dance, Barbara Mettler, Mettler Studios.
The New Ballet, Kurt Joss, A.V. Coton, Dennis Dobson Publishers.
Once Upon a Time, Arthur Rackham, Heinemann, London.
Oxford Book of Poetry for Children, Edward Blishen, Brian Wildsmith.
Pre-Classic Dance Forms, Louis Horst, Damin Dance Publishers.
Problems of Art, Susanne K. Langer, Charles Scribner's Sons.
The Poetic Image, C. Day Lewis, Jonathon Cape.
Poetry and Experience, Archibald MacLeish.
The Shape of Content, Ben Shahn, Harvard University Press.
The Sense of Beauty, Santayana, Dover Publications.
You Can Teach Creativity, Elizabeth Allstrom, Alungdon Press.
World History of the Dance, Curt Sachs, W. W. Norton.

Song of Myself
Photograph: Dieter Herrmann
for One Extra Dance Group
Choreography: Coralie Hinkley

Some students have continued
to dance after leaving school
namely with Margaret Barr;
One Extra Dance Group, and
Coralie Hinkley

The Bound Ones
Photograph: Dieter Herrmann
for One Extra Dance Group
Choreography: Coralie Hinkley